Helps to Happiness

MIZPAH

Thou goest thy way,
    and I go mine,
Apart, yet not afar;
Only a thin veil hangs between
    The pathways where we are.
"God keep watch 'tween
              thee and me";
    This is my prayer;
He looketh thy way,
           He looketh mine,
    And keeps us near.

Although our paths be separate,
    And thy way is not mine,
Yet coming to the mercy-seat,
    My soul will meet with thine.
"God keep watch 'tween
              thee and me"
    I'll whisper there;
He blesseth thee,
           He blesseth me,
    And we are near.

    Julia A. Baker

Class __ BJ 1481

Book _____ B85

Copyright Nº _____

COPYRIGHT DEPOSIT

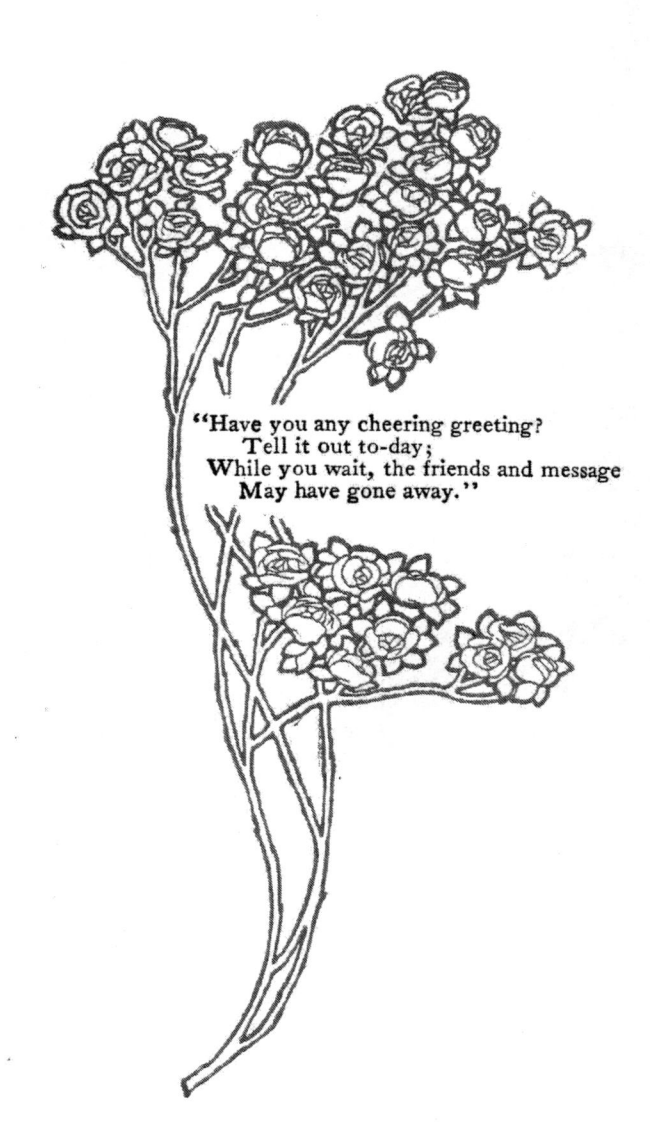

"Have you any cheering greeting?
 Tell it out to-day;
While you wait, the friends and message
 May have gone away."

Books of Helpful Thoughts

THOUGHTS. Compiled by Ladies of Fabiola Hospital Association. Cloth, $1.25; leather, $2.00.

FOR THY GOOD CHEER. Compiled by Ladies of Fabiola Hospital Association. Cloth, $1.25; leather, $2.00.

STRENGTH FOR EVERY DAY. A compilation of beautiful thoughts. Cloth, $1.25; leather, $2.00.

BORROWINGS. By the compilors of "Thoughts." Cloth, $1.25; leather, $2.00.

MORE BORROWINGS. Cloth, $1.25; leather, $2.00.

OUT OF DOORS. Compiled by Rosalie Arthur. Cloth, $1.25; leather, $2.00.

DODGE PUBLISHING COMPANY
220 EAST 23rd STREET, NEW YORK

HELPS TO HAPPINESS

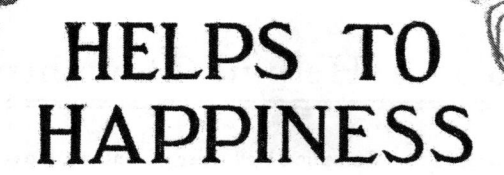

Selected and Arranged
by
RICHARD BROOKS

Blessed are the Happiness Makers. Blessed are they who know how to shine on one's gloom with their cheer. —Henry Ward Beecher.

New York
DODGE PUBLISHING COMPANY
220 East 23rd Street

The Compilor desires to thank the various authors and publishers who have so generously permitted the use of selections from works copyrighted by them.

Copyrighted, 1907, by
DODGE PUBLISHING COMPANY

The world is so full of a number of things I'm sure we should all be happy as kings

Robert Louis Stevenson

HELPS TO HAPPINESS

The idea has been transmitted from generation to generation, that happiness is one large and beautiful stone, a single gem so rare that all search after it is vain, all effort for it hopeless. It is not so. Happiness is mosaic, composed of many smaller stones. Each taken apart and viewed singly may be of little value; but when all are grouped together and judiciously combined and set, they form a pleasing and graceful whole—a costly jewel. Trample not under feet, then, the little pleasures which a gracious Providence scatters in the daily path, and which, in eager search after some great and exciting joy, we are apt to overlook. Why should we always keep our eyes fixed on the bright, distant horizon, while there are so many lovely roses in the garden in which we are permitted to walk? The very ardor of our chase after happiness may be the reason that she so often eludes our grasp.

If you ever find happiness by hunting for it, you will find it, as the old woman did her lost spectacles, safe on her own nose all the time.
—*Josh Billings.*

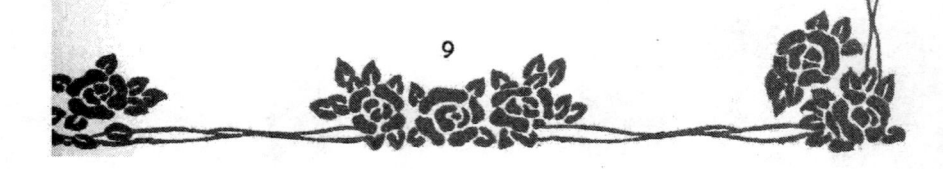

HELPS TO HAPPINESS

In Life's small things be resolute and great
To keep thy muscles trained; know'st thou when fate
Thy measure takes? or when she'll say to thee,
"I find thee worthy, do this thing for me!"
—*Emerson.*

"Put a seal upon your lips and forget what you have done. After you have been kind, after love hath stolen forth into the world and done its beautiful work, go back into the shade again and say nothing about it."

Love is not getting, but giving; not a wild dream of pleasure, and a madness of desire—oh, no, love is not that—it is goodness and honor, and peace and pure living—yes, love is that; and it is the best thing in the world, and the thing that lives longest.
—*Henry van Dyke.*

I will this day try to live a simple, sincere, and serene life; repelling promptly every thought of discontent, anxiety, discouragement, impurity, and self-seeking; cultivating cheerfulness, magnanimity, charity, and the habit of holy silence; exercising economy in expenditure, carefulness in conversation, diligence in appointed service, fidelity to every trust, and a childlike trust in God.   —*John H. Vincent.*

HELPS TO HAPPINESS

"Stay at home," said Inclination,
   "Let the errand wait."
"Go at once!" said Duty, firmly,
   "Or you'll be too late."

"But it snows," said Inclination,
   "And the wind is keen."
"Never mind all that," said Duty:
   "Go and brave it, Jean."

Jean stepped out into the garden,
   Look up at the sky,
Clouded, shrouded, dreary, sunless,
   Snow unceasingly.

"Stay!" again said Inclination,
   "Go!" said Duty, "Go!"
Forth went Jean with no more waiting,
   Forth into the snow.

You will smile if now I tell you,
   That this quiet strife,
Duty conquering Inclination,
   Strengthened all her life.

Sometimes on a little skirmish
   Hangs a nation's fate.
Very much hung on that skirmish
   At the garden gate.

HELPS TO HAPPINESS

Some men want to have religion like a dark lantern, and carry it in their pocket, where nobody but themselves can get any good from it.
—*Henry Ward Beecher.*

Try to care about something in this vast world besides the gratification of small selfish desires. Try to care for what is best in thought and action—something that is good apart from the accidents of your own lot. Look on other lives besides your own. See what their troubles are, and how they are borne. —*George Eliot.*

When friendships are real, they are not glass threads or frost work, but the solidest things we can know. —*Emerson.*

There is always hope in a man that actually and earnestly works. In idleness alone is there perpetual despair. . —*Thomas Carlyle.*

God has a few of us whom He whispers in the ear;
The rest may reason and welcome: 'tis we musicians *know.* —*Robert Browning.*

The knowledge which a man can use is the only real knowledge, the only knowledge which has life and growth in it, and converts itself into practical power.
—*James Anthony Froude.*

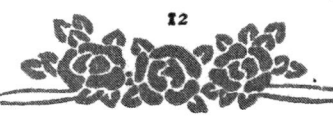

HELPS TO HAPPINESS

So night is grandeur to our dust,
   So near is God to man,
When Duty whispers low, Thou must,
   The youth replies, I can!
                   —*Emerson.*

It will be found everywhere that the men who have succeeded in business have been the men who have earnestly given themselves to it. Far more than mere talents or acquirements, enthusiasm and energy in work carry the day.
                   —*Tullock.*

"A young man idle, an old man needy."

"Nowhere is the goal of him who follows the route of Anywhere. The man who aims at nothing in particular invariably hits his mark."

"If you start a wagon down hill it goes itself, but if you want to go up hill you must keep a pushin' and a pullin'—it is the same way with your business."

He that despiseth little things, shall perish by little and little.   —*Solomon.*

If you would be pungent, be brief; for it is with words as with sunbeams—the more they are condensed the deeper they burn.
                   —*Southey.*

HELPS TO HAPPINESS

It is the easiest thing in the world for a man to deceive himself. —*Benjamin Franklin.*

The nature which is all wood and straw is of no use; if we are to do well, we must have some iron in us. —*Canon Farrar.*

Ever judge of men by their professions. For though the bright moment of promising is but a moment, and cannot be prolonged, yet if sincere in its moments, extravagant goodness, why, trust it, and know the man by it, I say—not by his performance; which is half the world's work, interfere as the world needs must with its accidents and circumstances: the profession was purely the man's own. I judge people by what they might be—not are, nor will be.
—*Robert Browning.*

No backward glance shall hinder or appall me;
    A new life is begun:
And better hopes and better motives call me
    Than those the past has won.
—*Lillian Knapp.*

All one's life is music if one touches the notes rightly and in tune. —*Ruskin.*

If you wish to be borne with yourself, bear with others. —*Thomas A. Kempis.*

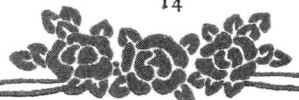

HELPS TO HAPPINESS

After all, what would life be without fighting, I should like to know? From the cradle to the grave, fighting, rightly understood, is the business, the real, highest, honestest business, of every son of man.

—*Thomas Hughes.*

HELPS TO HAPPINESS

The first thing a kindness deserves is acceptance; the second, transmission.
—*George MacDonald.*

Probably he who never made a mistake never made anything. —*Samuel Smiles.*

How much fretting might be prevented by a thorough conviction that there can be no such thing as unmixed good in this world!
—*Arthur Helps.*

Ability is of little account without opportunity.
—*Napoleon I.*

"All truth is from God, as all light is from the sun. . . All truth that bears on the culture of the human soul, the development of human life, is part of the unfolding revelation of the divine. So when we catch glimpses, intimations, ideals, of those things that are finer and better than have ever yet been incarnated in the life of the race, we are anticipating that which is to be written on those new leaves of God's book, to be clearly read when they shall be turned, in His ever progressive, always advancing, and never completed Bible."

To carry care to bed is to sleep with a pack on your back. —*Haliburton.*

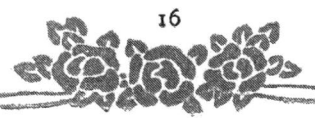

HELPS TO HAPPINESS

Be wise to-day; 'tis madness to defer;
Next day the fatal precedent will plead;
Thus on, till wisdom is pushed out of life.
Procrastination is the thief of time;
Year after year it steals, till all are fled,
And to the mercies of a moment leaves
The vast concerns of an eternal scene.
—*Edward Young.*

We meet at one gate
When all's over. The ways they are many and wide,
And seldom are two ways the same.
Side by side may we stand at the same little door when all's done!
The ways they are many, the end it is one.
—*Owen Meredith.*

The most I can do for my friend is simply to be his friend. I have no wealth to bestow upon him. If he knows that I am happy in loving him, he will want no other reward. Is not friendship divine in this?
—*Henry David Thoreau.*

If we accept the simple and unadulterated gospel of a Father's love, and it makes us fit to live and ready to die, we do well to leave that gospel to our children as a valuable and sacred inheritance.

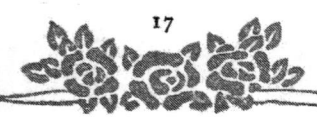

HELPS TO HAPPINESS

If you've any debt to pay,
   Rest you neither night nor **day:**
      Pay it.

It is better to kno less than to kno much that ain't so.   —*Josh Billings.*

They are never alone that are accompanied with noble thoughts.   —*Philip Sidney.*

Four things a man must learn to do
If he would make his record true:
To think without confusion clearly;
To love his fellow-men sincerely;
To act from honest motives purely;
To trust in God and heaven securely.
    —*Henry van Dyke.*

Most of the work of the world is drudgery. I have seen President Roosevelt performing all day nothing but drudgery, but he didn't realize it was drudgery. The men who succeed do not know that they are performing drudgery. Don't work for wages. Work for the accomplishment of something. God put into the human mind a desire to do something. It is godlike. God made the world; we must make or do something.   —*Leslie M. Shaw.*

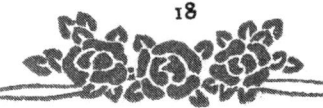

HELPS TO HAPPINESS

Keep your face always toward the sunshine and the shadows will fall behind you

M. B. Whitman

HELPS TO HAPPINESS

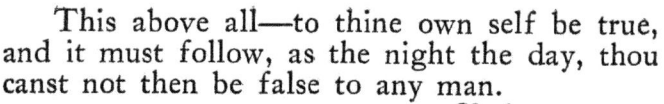

This above all—to thine own self be true, and it must follow, as the night the day, thou canst not then be false to any man.
—*Shakespeare.*

When a man has not a good reason for doing a thing, he has one good reason for letting it alone. —*Walter Scott.*

There can be no substitute for the world-old humdrum, commonplace qualities of truth, justice and courage, thrift, industry, common sense, and genuine sympathy with and fellow-feeling for others. —*Theodore Roosevelt.*

The man who cannot be strong, cheerful, creative, in his own age, would find all other ages inhospitable and barren.
—*Hamilton W. Mabie.*

You will find it a safe rule to take a thing just as quick as it is offered—especially a job. It is never easy to get one, except when you don't want it; but when you've got to get work, and go after it with a gun, you'll find it as shy as an old crow that every farmer in the county has shot at. —*George Horace Lorimer.*

HELPS TO HAPPINESS

Take time to speak a loving word
Where loving words are seldom heard;
And it will linger in the mind,
And gather others of its kind,
Till loving words will echo where
Erstwhile the heart was poor and bare;
And somewhere on thy heavenward track,
Their music will come echoing back,
And flood thy soul with melody,
Such is Love's immortality.

I expect to pass through this life but once. If therefore there is any kindness I can show, or any good I can do to any fellow-being, let me do it now; let me not defer or neglect it, for I shall not pass this way again.
—*A. B. Hegeman.*

If we stand idly by, if we seek merely swollen, slothful ease and ignoble peace, if we shrink from the hard contests where men must win at hazard of their lives and at risk of all they hold dear, then the bolder and stronger peoples will pass us by, and will win for themselves the domination of the world.
—*Theodore Roosevelt.*

There is nothing so strong or safe in an emergency of life as the simple truth.
—*Charles Dickens.*

HELPS TO HAPPINESS

We communicate happiness to others not often by great acts of devotion and self-sacrifice, but by the absence of fault-finding and censure, by being ready to sympathize with their notions and feelings, instead of forcing them to sympathize with ours.
—*James Freeman Clarke.*

Die when I may, I want it said of me, by those who knew me best, that I always plucked a thistle and planted a flower when I thought a flower would grow. —*Abraham Lincoln.*

Do the duty next to you, leave the rest to develop itself. —*F. W. Robertson.*

The absence of a poetic taste is a sad indication of a lack of the imaginative faculty; and without imagination what is life?
—*Richardson.*

What is good is worth repeating.
—*Plato.*

"Old wood to burn,
Old wine to drink
Old friends to trust,
Old books to read."

I am more and more impressed with the duty of finding happiness. —*George Eliot.*

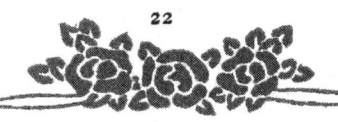

HELPS TO HAPPINESS

Take a dash of water cold
    And a little leaven of prayer,
A little bit of sunshine gold
    Dissolved in the morning air;
Add to your meal some merriment
    And a thought for kith and kin;
And then, as a prime ingredient,
    A plenty of work thrown in:
But spice it all with the essence of love
    And a little whiff of play:
Let a wise old book and a glance above
    Complete a well spent day.
    "Whenever you feel blue
    Something for some one else go do."

HELPS TO HAPPINESS

Tongues in trees,
Books in the running brooks,
Sermons in stones and good in everything.
—*W. S. Peace.*

Nay, falter not; 'tis an assured good
To seek the noblest; 'tis your only good
Now you have seen it, for the higher vision
Poisons all meaner choice for evermore.
—*George Eliot.*

"A noble soul is like a ship at sea,
That sleeps at anchor when the ocean's calm;
But when she rages, and the wind blows high,
He cuts his way with skill and majesty."

You surrender a dear friend at the call of death, and out of his grave the real power of friendship rises stronger and more eternal in your life. —*Phillips Brooks.*

A man lives by believing something, not by debating and arguing about many things.
—*Thomas Carlyle.*

Those who learn nothing, or accumulate nothing in life, are set down as failure because they have neglected little things.
—*Samuel Smiles.*

HELPS TO HAPPINESS

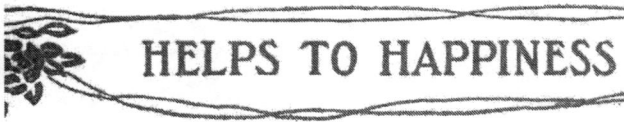

Our doubts are traitors,
And make us lose the good we often might win,
By fearing to attempt.
—*Shakespeare.*

To be true—first to myself—and just and merciful. To be kind and faithful in the little things. To be brave with the bad; openly grateful for good; always moderate. To seek the best, content with what I find—placing principles above persons and right above riches. Of fear, none; of pain, enough to make my joys stand out; of pity, some; of work, a plenty; of faith in God and man, much; of love, all.
—*Leigh Mitchell Hodges.*

Thy friends thou hast and their adoption tried,
Grapple them to thy soul with hoops of steel;
But do not dull thy palm with entertainment
Of each new-hatched, unfledged comrade.
—*Shakespeare.*

Repose we may possess even in the most arduous toil; ease we can never have while we are surrounded by conditions which are hostile to our highest life.
—*Hamilton W. Mabie.*

HELPS TO HAPPINESS

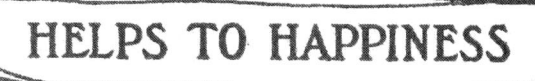

"Have you had a kindness shown?
    Pass it on,
'Twas not given for you alone—
    Pass it on.
Let it travel down the years,
Let it wipe another's tears,
'Till in heaven the deed appears—
    Pass it on."

A young man has always had to help make his opportunities, and he must do that to-day as ever. But young men fail more nowadays than they used to because they expect to reap almost as soon as they sow. That is the very great trouble with the young men of the present. They expect opportunities to come to them without application or proper shaping of things so that opportunities will drift their way. You have to keep your eyes open and catch hold of things; they'll not catch hold of you as a rule.
—*James J. Hill.*

HELPS TO HAPPINESS

Good taste is essentially a moral quality. Taste is not only a part of an index of morality—it is the only morality. The first, last, and closest trial question to any living creature is, "What do you like?"—and the entire object of true education is to make people not merely do right things, but enjoy the right things. What we like determines what we are, and is the sign of what we are; and to teach taste is inevitably to form character. —*Ruskin.*

Reflect upon your present blessings, of which every man has many; not on your past misfortunes, of which all men have some.
—*Charles Dickens.*

Friendship hath the skill and observation of the best physician, the diligence and vigilance of the best nurse, and the tenderness and patience of the best mother. —*Clarendon.*

The true Christian is the true citizen, lofty of purpose, resolute in endeavor, ready for a hero's deeds, but never looking down on his task because it is cast in the day of small things; scornful of baseness, awake to his own duties as well as to his rights, following the higher law with reverence and in this world doing all that in him lies, so that when death comes he may feel that mankind is in some degree better because he has lived. —*Theodore Roosevelt.*

HELPS TO HAPPINESS

I learned to cultivate the qualities of courage and patience when I was 16 years of age. Soon my employers knew that I wanted to do the right thing. Bankers came to have confidence in me, and then my success followed, step by step. —*John D. Rockefeller.*

Sleep sweetly in this quiet room,
  O thou, whoe'er thou art,
And let no mournful yesterdays
  Disturb thy peaceful heart.
  Nor let to-morrow scare thy rest
  With thoughts of coming ill;
Thy Maker is thy changeless friend,
  His love surrounds thee still.
Forget thyself and all the world;
  Put out each feverish light,
The stars are watching overhead,
  Sleep sweetly then. Good night.

HELPS TO HAPPINESS

Sir, my concern is not whether God is on our side; my great concern is to be on God's side, for God is always right.
—*Abraham Lincoln.*

HELPS TO HAPPINESS

He who helps a child helps humanity with a distinctness which no other help given to human creatures can possibly give. He who puts his influence into the fountain where the river comes out puts his influence in everywhere. No land it may not reach. —*Phillips Brooks.*

All true work is sacred; in all true work, even if but true hand-labor, there is something of divineness. O brother, if this is not worship, then I say the more pity for worship, for this is the noblest thing yet discovered under God's sky. Who are thou who complainest of thy life of toil? Complain not. Look up, my wearied brother: see thy fellow workmen there in God's eternity; surviving there, they alone surviving; sacred band of the immortals, celestial bodyguard of the Empire of Mankind. Even in the weak human memory they survive as saints, as heroes, as gods; they alone surviving, peopling they alone stand the unmeasured solitudes of time. To thee Heaven, though severe, is not unkind; Heaven is kind; as a noble mother, as that Spartan mother saying, when she gave her son his shield, With this, my son, or upon it. Thou, too, shalt return home in honour, to thy far distant home in honour, doubt it not, if in the battle thou keep thy shield.
—*Thomas Carlyle.*

HELPS TO HAPPINESS

Write it on your heart that every day is the best day in the year. No man has learned anything rightly until he knows that every day is Doomsday. To-day is a king in disguise. To-day always looks mean to the thoughtless, in the face of an uniform experience that all good and great and happy actions are made up precisely of these blank to-days. Let us not be so deceived; let us unmask the king as he passes.
—*Emerson.*

And one should give a gleam of happiness whenever it is possible. —*George Eliot.*

There is a race of narrow wits that never get rich for want of courage. Their understanding is of that halting, balancing kind which gives a man just enough light to see difficulties and start doubts, but not enough to surmount the one or to remove the other. They never get ahead an inch, because they are always hugging some coward maxim, which they can only interpret literally. "Never change a certainty for an uncertainty," "A bird in the hand is worth two in the bush," are their favorite saws; and very good ones they are, too, but not to be followed too slavishly. —*William Mathews.*

HELPS TO HAPPINESS

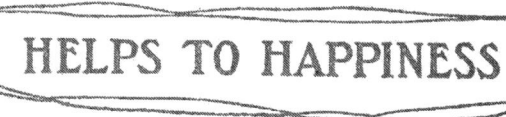

If you strike a thorn or rose,
    Keep a Goin'!
If it hails or if it snows
    Keep a Goin'!
'Tain't no use to sit and whine
When the fish ain't on your line,
Bait your hook and keep on tryin'—
    Keep a Goin'!

If the weather kills your crop
    Keep a Goin'!
When you tumble from the top
    Keep a Goin'!
S'pose you're out of every dime
Gettin' broke ain't any crime;
Tell the world you're feelin' prime—
    Keep a Goin'!

When it looks like all is up
    Keep a Goin'!
Drain the sweetness from the cup,
    Keep a Goin'!
See the wild birds on the wing,
Hear the bells that sweetly ring;
When you feel like sighin'—sing;
    Keep a Goin'!

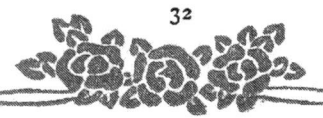

HELPS TO HAPPINESS

Words are things, and a small drop of ink
Falling like dew upon a thought, produces
That which makes thousands, perhaps millions,
    think.   —*Byron.*

Try to be happy in this present moment, and put not off being so to a time to come; as though that time should be of another make from this, which has already come, and is sure.
—*T. Fuller.*

Ask yourself what you would have been if you had never been tempted, and own what a blessed thing the educating power of temptation is.   —*Phillips Brooks.*

"Drop the subject when you cannot agree; there is no need to be bitter because you know you are right."

"And he who serves his brother best,
  Gets nearer God than all the rest."

We make way for the man who boldly pushes past us.   —*Bovee.*

Whoever you are, I earnestly entreat you to dispatch your business as soon as possible, and then depart, unless you come hither, like another Hercules, to lend some friendly assistance, for here will be work to employ you and as many as enter this place.   —*Aldus Pius Manutius.*

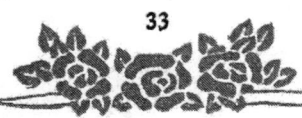

HELPS TO HAPPINESS

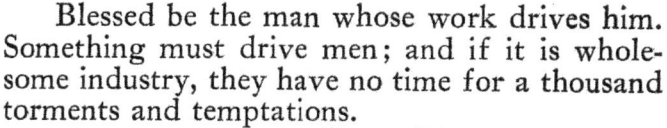

Blessed be the man whose work drives him. Something must drive men; and if it is wholesome industry, they have no time for a thousand torments and temptations.
—*Henry Ward Beecher.*

Labor to keep alive in your breast that little spark of celestial fire called Conscience.
—*George Washington.*

I believe that this matter of specialization is already—and as the years pass will become more and more—the keynote of success. The world's effective workers are constantly increasing in number. Competition is growing steadily keener. To win recognition a man will have to do one thing extremely well. If I were giving just one word of advice to a young man I should say—concentrate. —*Alfred Harmsworth.*

Do not conclude that a man is modest because he lowers his eyes before eulogy. Observe, rather, whether he holds his head high before just criticism. —*Charles Wagner.*

Give us, give us, the man who sings at his work! Be his occupation what it may, he is equal to any of those who follow the same pursuit in silent sullenness. He does more in the same time—he will do it better—he will persevere longer. —*Thomas Carlyle.*

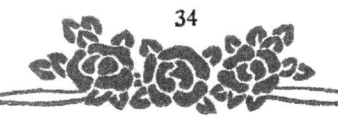

HELPS TO HAPPINESS

This is peace:
To conquer love of self and lust of life,
To tear deep-rooted passion from the heart,
To still the inward strife;

For love to clasp Eternal Beauty close;
For glory to be Lord of self; for pleasure
To live beyond the gods; for countless wealth
To lay up lasting treasure.

Of perfect service rendered, duties done
In charity, soft speech, and stainless days:
These riches shall not fade away in life,
Nor any death dispraise.

Then Sorrow ends, for Life and Death have ceased;
How should lamps flicker when their oil is spent?
The old sad count is clear, the new is clean;
Thus hath a man content.
—*Edwin Arnold.*

HELPS TO HAPPINESS

They who love best need friendship most;
  Hearts only thrive on varied good;
And he who gathers from a host
  Of friendly hearts his daily food,
Is the best friend that we can boast.
—*J. G. Holland.*

To be glad of life because it gives you the chance to love and to work and to play and to look up at the stars; to be satisfied with your possessions but not contented with yourself until you have made the best of them; to despise nothing in the world except falsehood and meanness, and to fear nothing except cowardice; to be governed by your admirations rather than by your disgusts; to covet nothing that is your neighbor's except his kindness of heart and gentleness of manners; to think seldom of your enemies, often of your friend, and every day of Christ; and to spend as much time as you can with body and with spirit, in God's out-of-doors—these are little guide-posts on the foot-path to peace. —*Henry van Dyke.*

What is useful is beautiful.
—*Socrates.*

Hundreds can talk to one who can think; thousands can think to one who can see.
—*Ruskin.*

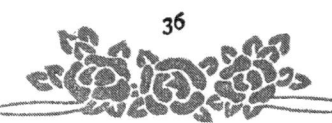

HELPS TO HAPPINESS

I shall pass this way but once any good thing, therefore that I can do or any kindness that I can show to any human being, let me do it now Let me not defer it nor neglect it for I shall not pass this way again

A. B. Hegeman

HELPS TO HAPPINESS

Simplicity is less dependent upon external things than we imagine. It can live in broadcloth or homespun; it can eat white bread or black. It is not outward, but inward. A certain openness of mind to learn the daily lessons of life; a certain willingness of heart to give and to receive that extra service, that gift beyond the strict measure of debt which makes friendship possible; a certain clearness of spirit to perceive the best in things and people, to love it without fear and to cleave to it without mistrust; a peaceable sureness of affection and taste; a gentle straightforwardness of action; a kind sincerity of speech,—these are the marks of the simple life, which is within. I have seen it in a hut. I have seen it in a palace. And wherever it is found it is the best prize of the school life, the badge of a scholar well-beloved of the Master.

—Henry van Dyke.

HELPS TO HAPPINESS

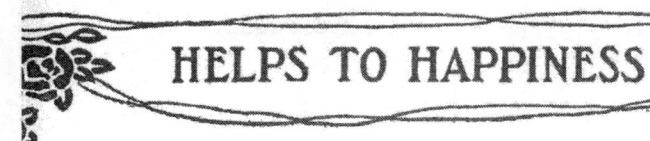

For life, with all it yields of joy or woe
      And hope and fear,
Is just our chance o' the prize of learning love—
How love might be, hath been, indeed, and is.
                —Robert Browning.

HELPS TO HAPPINESS

So let my past stand just as it stands,
   And let me now, as I may grow old.
I am what I am, and my life for me
   Is the best, or it had not been, I hold.
—*P. Carey.*

If we have not quiet in our minds, outward comfort will do no more for us than a golden slipper on a gouty foot.   —*John Bunyan.*

One example is worth a thousand arguments.
—*Gladstone.*

Labor rids us of three great evils: tediousness, vice and poverty.   —*French.*

To be honest, to be kind, to earn a little, and to spend a little less, to make, upon the whole, a family happier for his presence, to renounce when that shall be necessary and not to be embittered, to keep a few friends, but these without capitulation; above all, on the same condition, to keep friends with himself: here is a task for all a man has of fortitude and delicacy.
—*Robert Louis Stevenson.*

In this world, it is not what we take up, but what we give up, that makes us rich.
—*Henry Ward Beecher.*

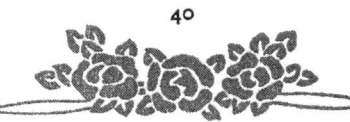

HELPS TO HAPPINESS

If a man is unhappy this must be his own fault; for God made all men to be happy.
—*Epictetus.*

It is a good and safe rule to sojourn in every place, as if you meant to spend your life there, never omitting an opportunity of doing a kindness, or speaking a true word, or making a friend. —*Ruskin.*

There may be doubts, however, as to which was using his time best. The one could afford time to think, and the other never could. The one could have sympathies and do kindnesses, and the other must needs be always selfish. He could not cultivate a friendship or do a charity, or admire a work of genius, or kindle at the sight of beauty or the sound of a sweet song— he had no time, and no eyes for anything but his law books. All was dark outside his reading lamp. Love and Nature and Art . . . were shut out from him. —*Thackeray.*

Every day should be passed as if it were to be our last. —*Publius Syrus.*

Three things are necessary for success— first, backbone; second, backbone; third, backbone. —*Charles Sumner.*

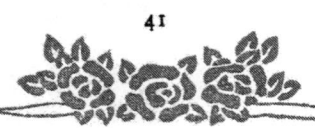

HELPS TO HAPPINESS

Live not without a friend: the Alpine rock must own
Its mossy grace or else be nothing but a stone.
—*W. W. Story.*

The day returns and brings us the petty round of irritating concerns and duties. Help us to play the man, help us to perform them with laughter and kind faces; let cheerfulness abound with industry. Give us to go blithely on our business all this day, bring us to our resting beds weary and content and undishonored; and grant us in the end the gift of sleep. Amen.
—*Robert Louis Stevenson.*

And it is only they who are faithful in a few things who will be faithful over many things; only they who do their duty in everyday and trivial matters who will fulfill them on great occasions.
—*Edwin Arnold.*

Blessed are they who have the gift of making friends, for it is one of God's best gifts. It involves many things, but, above all, the power of going out of one's self, and seeing and appreciating whatever is noble and loving in another.
—*Thomas Hughes.*

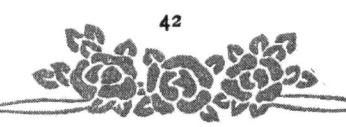

HELPS TO HAPPINESS

THE NATION'S PRAYER

God give us men! A time like this demands
Strong minds, great hearts, true faith, and ready
    hands.
Men whom the lust of office does not kill;
    Men whom the spoils of office cannot buy;
Men who possess opinions and a will;
    Men who have honor, and who will not lie;
Men who can stand before a demagogue
    And scorn his treacherous flatteries without
    winking.
Tall men, sun-crowned, who live above the fog
    In public duty and in private thinking!
                     —*J. G. Holland.*

HELPS TO HAPPINESS

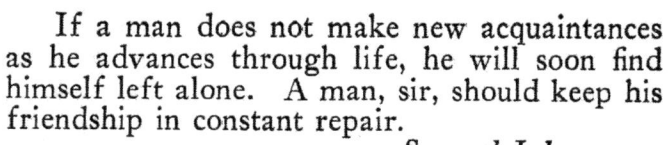

If a man does not make new acquaintances as he advances through life, he will soon find himself left alone. A man, sir, should keep his friendship in constant repair.
—*Samuel Johnson.*

HELPS TO HAPPINESS

Go to your friend for sympathy; that is natural. Go to your books for comfort, for counsel. But the time will come when no book, no friend, can decide your problem for you; when nothing can help you, nothing can save you, but yourself. Begin now to stand alone.
—*Angela Morgan.*

"Happiness is where it is found, and seldom where it is sought."

We beseech Thee, Lord, to behold us with favour, folk of many families and nations, gathered together in the peace of this roof. Be patient still; suffer us awhile longer to endure, and (if it may be), help us to do better. Bless to us our extraordinary mercies. Be with our friends; be with ourselves. Go with each of us to rest. If any awake, temper to them the dark hours of watching; and when the day returns to us, call us up with morning faces and with morning hearts—eager to labour—eager to be happy, if happiness shall be our portion—and if the day be marked for sorrow—strong to endure it. —*Robert Louis Stevenson.*

HELPS TO HAPPINESS

Everybody likes and respects self-made men. It is a great deal better to be made in that way than not at all. —*Holmes.*

There's nae power in Heaven or airth like love. It makes the weak strong and the dumb tae speak. —*Ian Maclaren.*

So long as we love, we serve; so long as we are loved by others I would almost say that we are indispensable; and no man is useless while he has a friend. —*Robert Louis Stevenson.*

Reputation is what men and women think of us; character is what God and the angels know of us. —*Thomas Paine.*

Give love, and love to *your* heart will flow,
  A strength in your utmost need;
Have faith, and a score of hearts will show
  Their faith in *your* work and deed.
    So others shall
Take patience, labor, to their heart and hand,
From thy hand and thy heart, and they brave
    cheer,
And God's grace fructify through thee to all.
—*Elizabeth Barrett Browning.*

HELPS TO HAPPINESS

LIFE'S MIRROR.

There are loyal hearts, there are spirits brave,
    There are souls that are pure and true;
Then give to the world the best you have,
    And the best will come back to you.

Give love, and love to your life will flow,
    A strength in your utmost need;
Have faith, and a score of hearts will show
    Their faith in your word and deed.

Give truth, and your gift will be paid in kind,
    And honor will honor meet;
And a smile that is sweet will surely find
    A smile that is just as sweet.

For life is the mirror of king and slave,
    'Tis just what we are and do;
Then give to the world the best you have,
    And the best will come back to you.
                  —Madeline S. Bridges.

HELPS TO HAPPINESS

Be humble or you'll stumble.
—*D. L. Moody.*

It matters not how strait the gate,
  How charged with punishments the scroll;
I am the master of my fate;
  I am the captain of my soul.
—*W. E. Henley.*

Few will at first be pleased with those thoughts which are entirely new to them, and which, if true, they feel to be truths which they should never have discovered for themselves.
—*Arthur Helps.*

The little worries which we meet each day
May lie as stumbling-blocks across our way,
Or we may make them stepping-stones to be
  Of grace, O Lord, to Thee.
—*Anna E. Hamilton.*

Nothing is more significant of men's character than what they find laughable.
—*Goethe.*

It is not required of every man and woman to be or to do something great; most of us must content ourselves with taking small parts in the chorus, as far as possible without discord.
—*Henry van Dyke.*

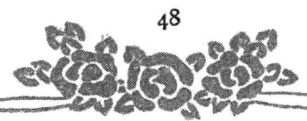

HELPS TO HAPPINESS

Believe in yourself believe in humanity, believe in the success of your undertakings Fear nothing and no one Love your work Work hope trust Keep in touch with to-day Teach yourself to be practical and up-to-date and sensible You cannot fail."

HELPS TO HAPPINESS

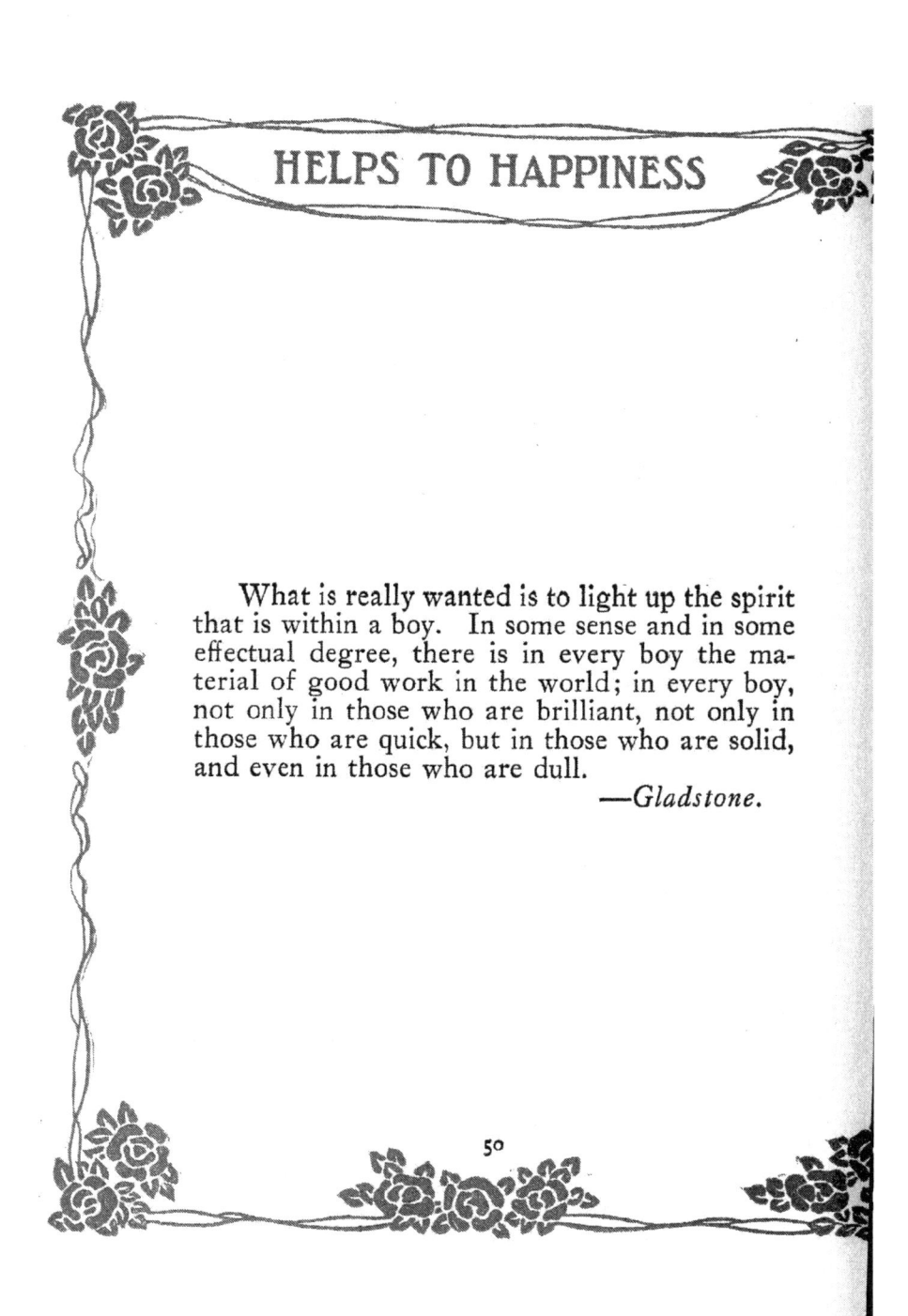

What is really wanted is to light up the spirit that is within a boy. In some sense and in some effectual degree, there is in every boy the material of good work in the world; in every boy, not only in those who are brilliant, not only in those who are quick, but in those who are solid, and even in those who are dull.

—*Gladstone.*

HELPS TO HAPPINESS

Adversity is sometimes hard upon a man; but for one man who can stand prosperity there are a hundred that will stand adversity.
—*Thomas Carlyle.*

Avoid excess in everything.
—*Socrates.*

It may be proved with much certainty that God intends no man to live in this world without working; but it seems to me no less evident that He intends every man to be happy in his work. It is written: "In the sweat of thy brow," but it was never written—"in the breaking of thine heart"—"thou shalt eat bread." I find that no small misery is caused by overworked and unhappy people, in the dark views which they necessarily take up themselves and force upon others of work itself. I believe the fact of their being unhappy is in itself a violation of divine law and a sign of some kind of folly or sin in their way of life. Now, in order that people may be happy in their work, these three things are needed: They must be fit for it; they must not do too much of it; and they must have a sense of success in it.
—*Ruskin.*

HELPS TO HAPPINESS

Thy love shall chant its own beatitudes
After its own self-working. A child's kiss
Set on thy sighing lips shall make thee glad;
A poor man served by thee shall make thee rich;
A sick man helped by thee shall make thee strong;
Thou shalt be served thyself by every sense
Of service which thou renderest
        —Elizabeth Barrett Browning.

Be not simply good—be good for something.
        —Henry David Thoreau.

HELPS TO HAPPINESS

Now is the time; ah, friend, no longer wait
To scatter loving smiles and words of cheer
To those around whose lives are now so dear.
They may not meet you in the coming year.
   Now is the time.

Keep the upward windows open. Do not dare to think that a child of God can worthily work out his career, or worthily serve God's other children, unless he does both in the love and fear of God their Father.
—*Phillips Brooks.*

Every honest occupation to which a man sets his hand would raise him into a philosopher, if he mastered all the knowledge that belonged to his craft. —*James Anthony Froude.*

The way to wealth is as plain as the way to market. It depends chiefly on two words—industry and frugality.
—*Benjamin Franklin.*

Dare to look up to God and say: "Make use of me for the future as Thou wilt. I am of the same mind; I am one with Thee. I refuse nothing which seems good to Thee. Lead me whither Thou wilt. Clothe me in whatever dress Thou wilt." —*Epictetus.*

When is man strong until he feels alone?
—*Robert Browning.*

HELPS TO HAPPINESS

It is not a question of how *much* we are to do, but of how it is to be done; it is not a question of doing more, but of doing better.
—*Ruskin.*

Let those who thoughtfully consider the brevity of life remember the length of eternity.
—*Bishop Ken.*

I hold every man a debtor to his profession; from the which as men of course do seek to receive countenance and profit, so ought they of duty to endeavour themselves by way of amends to be a help and ornament thereunto.
—*Bacon.*

Do not be troubled because you have not great virtues. God made a million spears of grass where he made one tree. The earth is fringed and carpeted, not with forests, but with grasses. Only have enough of little virtues and common fidelities, and you need not mourn because you are neither a hero nor a saint.
—*Henry Ward Beecher.*

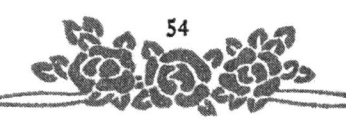

HELPS TO HAPPINESS

Build a little fence of trust around to-day,
Fill the space with loving works and therein stay;
Look not through the sheltering bars upon to-morrow;
God will help thee bear what comes of joy or sorrow. —*Mary Frances Butts.*

HELPS TO HAPPINESS

Think of living! Thy life, wert thou the pitifullest of all the sons of earth, is no idle dream, but a solemn reality. It is thy own. It is all thou hast to front eternity with. Work, then, even as He has done, and does, like a star, unhasting yet unresting.—*Thomas Carlyle.*

Religion is the best armor in the world; but the worst cloak. —*John Bunyan.*

Tell me with whom thou art found, and I will tell thee who thou art. —*Goethe.*

Let us learn to be content with what we have; let us get rid of our false estimates, set up all the higher ideals—a quiet home; vines of our own planting; a few books full of the inspiration of a genius; a few friends worthy of being loved and able to love us in return; a hundred innocent pleasures that bring no pain or remorse; a devotion to the right that will never swerve; a simple religion empty of all bigotry, full of trust and hope and love—and to such a philosophy this world will give up all the empty joy it has. —*David Swing.*

You cannot dream yourself into a character; you must hammer and forge yourself one.
—*James Anthony Froude.*

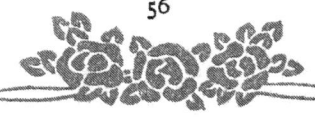

HELPS TO HAPPINESS

THE HUMAN TOUCH.

High thoughts and noble in all lands
  Help me. My soul is fed by such.
But, ah, the touch of lips and hands,
  The human touch!
Warm, vital, close, life's symbols dear:
These need I most, and now and here.
              —Richard Burton.

HELPS TO HAPPINESS

Why shouldst thou fill to-day with sorrow,
    About to-morrow,
        My heart?
One watches all with care most true,
Doubt not that He will give thee, too,
        Thy part.
—*Paul Fleming.*

Let not another's disobedience to Nature become an ill to you; for you were not born to be depressed and unhappy with others, but to be happy with them. And if any is unhappy, remember that he is so for himself; for God made all men to enjoy felicity and peace.
—*Epictetus.*

There is an idea abroad among moral people that they should make their neighbours good. One person I have to make good: myself. But my duty to my neighbour is much more nearly expressed by saying that I have to make him happy—if I may.
—*Robert Louis Stevenson.*

All service ranks the same with God,
With God whose puppets, best and worse,
Are we; there is no last nor first.
—*Robert Browning.*

HELPS TO HAPPINESS

Do not think it wasted time to submit yourselves to any influence which may bring upon you any noble feeling. —*Ruskin.*

A happy man or woman is a better thing to find than a five-pound note. He or she is a radiating focus of good will; and their entrance into a room is as though another candle had been lighted. He need not care whether they could prove the forty-seventh proposition; they do a better thing than that—they practically demonstrate the great theorem of the Livableness of Life. —*Robert Louis Stevenson.*

It is not written, blessed is he that feedeth the poor, but he that considereth the poor. A little thought and a little kindness are often worth more than a great deal of money.
—*Ruskin.*

To me there is no duty we so much underrate as the duty of being happy.
—*Robert Louis Stevenson.*

HELPS TO HAPPINESS

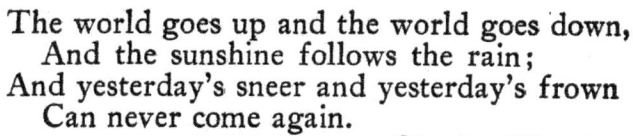

The world goes up and the world goes down,
    And the sunshine follows the rain;
And yesterday's sneer and yesterday's frown
    Can never come again.
                —*Charles Kingsley.*

It is worth a thousand pounds a year to have the habit of looking on the bright side of things.
                 —*Samuel Johnson.*

Remember there's always a voice saying the right thing to you somewhere if you'll only listen for it.   —*Thomas Hughes.*

There are thousands willing to do great things for one willing to do a small thing.
                 —*George MacDonald.*

There are many attorneys, but few lawyers; many doctors, but few physicians; many pedagogues, but few teachers; many storekeepers, but few merchants. Our country has reached the stage where it will pay any price for excellence. It is able and willing to do it. There are more ten-thousand-dollar jobs than there are ten-thousand-dollar men to take them. Of course there are men who would gladly take them, but the men with the capacity are few. First secure excellence, then set your price; the world will pay it.   —*Leslie M. Shaw.*

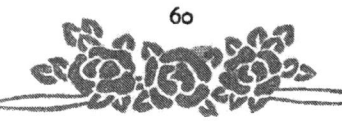

HELPS TO HAPPINESS

Nothing in this world comes to people who will not work. Nothing worth having comes to those who do not or are not willing to make an effort to get it. —*Theodore Roosevelt.*

People will remember the shining of the sun long after they have forgotten the thunderstorm. —*Ian Maclaren.*

I cannot think but that the world would be better and brighter if our teachers would dwell on the Duty of Happiness as well as the Happiness of Duty. —*F. Lubbock.*

Let us therefore boldly face the life of strife, resolute to do our duty well and manfully; resolute to uphold righteousness by deed and by word; resolute to be both honest and brave, to serve high ideals, yet to use practical methods.
—*Theodore Roosevelt.*

If I were to give advice, I would say: Begin at the bottom of the ladder; but be sure your ladder reaches above the basement. Don't try to get second-story pay for basement work. You will be lifted from the basement up higher if you are faithful. It makes little difference what you do, provided you do it better than it is done now. —*Leslie M. Shaw.*

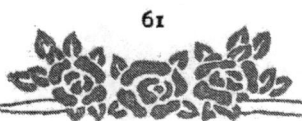

HELPS TO HAPPINESS

WAITING.

Serene, I fold my hands and wait,
   Nor care for wind, nor tide, nor sea;
I rave no more 'gainst time or fate,
   For lo! my own shall come to me.

I stay my haste, I make delays,
   For what avails this eager pace?
I stand amid the eternal ways,
   And what is mine shall know my face.

Asleep, awake, by night or day,
   The friends I seek are seeking me;
No wind can drive my bark astray,
   Nor change the tide of destiny.

What matter if I stand alone?
   I wait with joy the coming years;
My heart shall reap where it hath sown,
   And garner up its fruits of tears.

The waters know their own and draw
   The brook that springs in yonder heights;
So flows the good with equal law
   Unto the soul of pure delights.

The stars come nightly to the sky;
   The tidal wave unto the sea;
Nor time, nor space, nor deep, nor high,
   Can keep my own away from me.

                —*John Burroughs.*

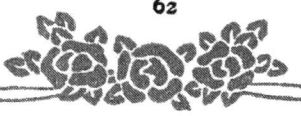

HELPS TO HAPPINESS

Her voice was ever soft,
Gentle, and low—an excellent thing in woman.
—*Shakespeare.*

Absence of occupation is not rest,
A mind quite vacant is a mind distressed.
—*Cowper.*

I wish to preach, not the doctrine of ignoble ease, but the doctrine of the strenuous life—the life of toil and effort, of labor and strife; to preach that highest form of success which comes, not to the man who desires mere easy peace, but to the man who does not shrink from danger, from hardship, or from bitter toil, and who out of these wins the splendid ultimate triumph.
—*Theodore Roosevelt.*

Aggressive fighting for the right is the greatest sport the world knows.
—*Theodore Roosevelt.*

In the hour of distress and misery the eye of every mortal turns to friendship: in the hour of gladness and conviviality, what is your want? It is friendship. When the heart overflows with gratitude, or with any other sweet and sacred sentiment, what is the word to which it would give utterance? A friend.
—*W. S. Landor.*

HELPS TO HAPPINESS

He that is down needs fear no fall,
 He that is low, no pride;
He that is humble ever shall
 Have God to be his guide.

I am content with what I have,
 Little be it or much;
And, Lord, contentment still I crave,
 Because thou savest such.

Fullness to such a burden is
 That go on pilgrimage;
Here little, and hereafter bliss,
 Is best from age to age.
—*John Bunyan.*

HELPS TO HAPPINESS

That low man seeks a little thing to do,
    Sees it and does it;
This high man, with a great thing to pursue,
    Dies ere he knows it.
That low man goes on adding one to one—
    His hundred's soon hit;
This high man, aiming at a million,
    Misses an unit.
That has the world here—should he need the next,
    Let the world mind him!
This throws himself on God, and unperplexed
    Seeking shall find him.
                —*Robert Browning.*

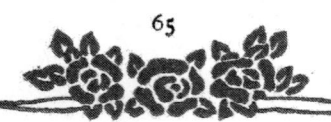

HELPS TO HAPPINESS

Is thy friend angry with thee? Then provide him an opportunity of showing thee a great favor. Over that his heart must needs melt, and he will love thee again. —*Richter.*

I have never united myself to any church, because I have found difficulty in giving my assent, without mental reservation, to the long complicated statements of Christian doctrine which characterize their Articles of Belief and Confession of Faith. Whenever any church will inscribe over its altar, as its sole qualification for membership, the Savior's condensed statement of the substance of both law and gospel, "Thou shalt love the Lord thy God with all thy heart, and with all thy soul, and with all thy mind, and thy neighbor as thyself," that church will I join with all my heart and all my soul.
—*Abraham Lincoln.*

When you have a number of disagreeable duties to perform, always do the most disagreeable first. —*Josiah Quincy.*

No pain, no palm; no thorns, no throne; no gall, no glory; no cross, no crown.
—*William Penn.*

HELPS TO HAPPINESS

If we could all see, and always see, the essential force which is in every good act, however slight it is, and in every true belief, however meagre it is, how different our lives would be.
—*Phillips Brooks.*

Everything that is mine, even to my life, I may give to one I love, but the secret of my friend is not mine to give.
—*Philip Sidney.*

There is a great difference between a young man looking for a situation and one looking for work. —*Leslie M. Shaw.*

Joy on, joy on, the foot-path road,
   And merrily trip the stile-a;
Your merry heart goes all the day,
   Your sad one tires in a mile-a.
—*Shakespeare.*

He jests at scars that never felt a wound.
—*Shakespeare.*

Nothing in this world comes to people who will not work. Nothing worth having comes to those who do not or are not willing to make an effort to get it. —*Theodore Roosevelt.*

HELPS TO HAPPINESS

Of course what we have a right to expect from the American boy is that he shall turn out to be a good American man. Now, the chances are strong that he won't be much of a man unless he is a good deal of a boy. He must not be a coward or a weakling, a bully, a shirk or a prig. He must work hard and play hard. He must be clean-minded and clean-lived, and able to hold his own under all circumstances and against all comers. It is only on these conditions that he will grow into the kind of a man of whom America can really be proud. In life as in a football game the principle to follow is: Hit the line hard; don't foul and don't shirk, but hit the line hard.

—*Theodore Roosevelt.*

HELPS TO HAPPINESS

There is nothing that we can properly call our own but our time, and yet everybody fools us out of it who has a mind to do it. If a man borrows a paltry sum of money, there must needs be bonds and securities, and every common civility is presently charged upon account. But he who has my time thinks he owes me nothing for it, though it be a debt that gratitude itself can never repay. —*Seneca.*

There shall never be one lost good! What was,
    shall live as before;
  The evil is null, is naught, is silence implying
    sound;
What was good shall be good, with, for evil so
    much good more;
  On the earth the broken arcs; in the heaven
    a perfect round.
                    —*Robert Browning.*

To have what we want is riches; but to be able to do without is power.
                 —*George MacDonald.*

Great privileges never go save in company with grave responsibilities.
                 —*Hamilton W. Mabie.*

HELPS TO HAPPINESS

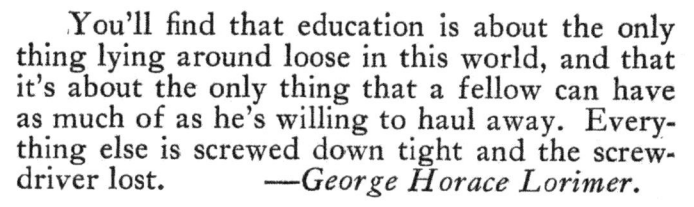

You'll find that education is about the only thing lying around loose in this world, and that it's about the only thing that a fellow can have as much of as he's willing to haul away. Everything else is screwed down tight and the screwdriver lost. —*George Horace Lorimer.*

Only grant my soul may carry high through death her cup unspilled,
Brimming though it be with knowledge, life's loss drop by drop distilled,
I shall boast it mine—the balsam, bless each kindly wrench that wrung
From life's tree its inmost virtue, tapped the root whence pleasures sprung,
Barked the bole, and broke the bough, and bruised the berry, left all grace
Ashes in death's stern alembic, loosed elixir in its place!
—*Robert Browning.*

No one is useless in the world who lightens the burden of it for any one else.
—*Charles Dickens.*

The bird that flutters least is longest on the wing. —*Cowper.*

We hardly find any persons of good sense, save those who agree with us.
—*La Rochefoucauld.*

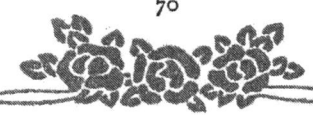

HELPS TO HAPPINESS

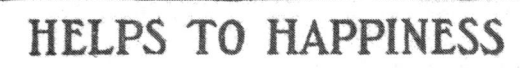

Knowing ourselves, our world, our task so great,
Our time so brief, 'tis clear if we refuse
The means so limited, the tools so rude
To execute our purpose, life will fleet,
And we shall fade, and leave our task undone.
We will be wise in time: what though our work
Be fashioned in despite of their ill-service,
Be crippled every way? 'Twere little praise
Did full resources wait on our good will
At every turn. Let all be as it is.
—*Robert Browning.*

Whatever I have tried to do in my life, I have tried with all my heart to do well. What I have devoted myself to, I have devoted myself to completely. Never to put one hand to anything on which I would throw my whole self, and never to affect depreciation of my work, whatever it was, I find now to have been golden rules. —*Charles Dickens.*

May all go well with you! May life's short day glide on peaceful and bright, with no more clouds than may glisten in the sunshine, no more rain than may form a rainbow.
—*Richter.*

HELPS TO HAPPINESS

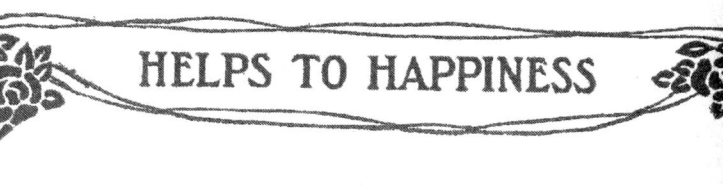

A FRIEND.

Deliberate long before thou consecrate a friend; and when thy impartial judgment concludes him worthy of thy bosom, receive him joyfully and entertain him wisely; impart thy secrets boldly, and mingle thy thoughts with his; he is thy very self: and use him so; if thou firmly believe him faithful, thou makest him so.
—*F. Quarles.*

HELPS TO HAPPINESS

Believe nothing against another but on good authority; nor report what may hurt another, unless it be a greater hurt to conceal it.
—*William Penn.*

"We pardon in the degree that we love."

If any man can convince me and bring home to me that I do not think or act aright, gladly will I change; for I search after truth, by which man never yet was harmed. But he is harmed who abideth on still in his deception and ignorance. —*Marcus Aurelius.*

Clothe with life the weak intent,
Let me be the thing I meant,
Let me find in Thy employ
Peace that dearer is than joy,
Out of self to love be led,
And to heaven acclimated,
Until all things sweet and good
Seem my natural habitude.
—*John G. Whittier.*

Go often to the house of thy friend; for weeds soon choke up the unused path.
—*Scandinavian proverb.*

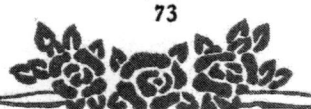

HELPS TO HAPPINESS

Seek not to pour the world into thy little mould,
Each as its nature is, its being must unfold;
Thou art but as a string in life's vast sounding board,
And other strings as sweet will not with thine accord.
—*W. W. Story*.

HELPS TO HAPPINESS

Never hunt trouble. However dead a shot one may be, the gun he carries on such expeditions is sure to kick, or go off half-cocked.
—*Artemus Ward.*

We are firm believers in the maxim, that for all right judgment of any man or thing it is useful, nay, essential, to see his good qualities before pronouncing on his bad.
—*Thomas Carlyle.*

What are you worth to-day? Not in money, but in brains, heart, purpose, character? Tell yourself the truth about yourself.
—*George H. Hepworth.*

The law of worthy life is . . . fundamentally the law of strife. . . . It is only through labor and painful effort, by grim energy and resolute courage, that we move on to better things. —*Theodore Roosevelt.*

Have no fear of robbers or murderers. Such dangers are from without, and are but petty. We should fear ourselves. Prejudices are the real robbers; vices the real murderers. The great dangers are within us.
—*Victor Hugo.*

Every brave heart must treat society as a child, and never allow it to dictate.
—*Emerson.*

HELPS TO HAPPINESS

To keep my health!
To do my work!
To live!
To see to it I grow and gain and give!
Never to look behind me for an hour!
To wait in weakness, and to walk in power;
But always fronting onward to the light,
Always and always facing toward the right,
Robbed, starved, defeated, fallen, wide astray—
On, with what strength I have!
Back to the way!
—*Charlotte Perkins Stetson.*

HELPS TO HAPPINESS

Whichever way the wind doth blow
Some heart is glad to have it so;
Then blow it east or blow it west,
The wind that blows that wind is best.
—*C. A. Mason.*

It does not take great men to do great things; it only takes consecrated men.
—*Phillips Brooks.*

Who has the clearest and intensest vision of what is at issue in the great battle of life, and who quits himself in it most manfully, will be the first to acknowledge that for him there has been no approach to victory except by the faithful doing day by day of the work which lay at his own threshold. —*Thomas Hughes.*

"A friend may well be reckoned a masterpiece of nature."

To work, to help and to be helped, to learn sympathy through suffering, to learn faith by perplexity, to reach truth through wonder,—behold! this is what it is to prosper, this is what it is to live. —*Phillips Brooks.*

HELPS TO HAPPINESS

"He that brings sunshine into the lives of others cannot keep it from himself."

"This world is a difficult world indeed,
   And people are hard to suit,
And the man who plays on the violin
   Is a bore to the man with a flute."

"I would flood your path with sunshine; I would fence you from all ill;
I would crown you with all blessings, if I could but have my will;
Aye! but human love may err, dear, and a power all wise is near;
So I only pray, God bless you, and God keep you through the year."

HELPS TO HAPPINESS

If I have faltered more or less
In my great task of happiness;
If I have moved among my race
And shown no glorious morning face;
If beams from happy human eyes
Have moved me not; if morning skies,
Books, and my food, and summer rain
Knocked on my sullen heart in vain;
Lord, Thy most pointed pleasure take,
And stab my spirit broad awake.

—Robert Louis Stevenson.

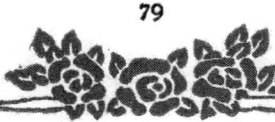

HELPS TO HAPPINESS

Make yourself necessary to somebody.
—*Emerson.*

Do not look forward to what might happen to-morrow; the same everlasting Father who cares for you to-day will take care of you to-morrow, and every day. Either He will shield you from suffering, or He will give you unfailing strength to bear it. Be at peace, then, and put aside all anxious thoughts and imaginations. —*St. Francis de Sales.*

He that cannot think, is a fool;
He that will not, is a bigot;
He that dare not, is a slave.
Inscription on the wall of Andrew Carnegie's Library.

"A little thing, a sunny smile,
A loving word at morn.
 And all day long the day shone bright,
 The cares of life were made more light,
And sweetest hopes were born."

Much of our dissension is due to misunderstanding, which could be put right by a few honest words and a little open dealing.
—*Black.*

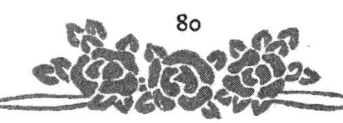

HELPS TO HAPPINESS

This truth comes to us more and more the longer we live: that on what field or in what uniform or with what aims we do our duty, matters very little, or even what our duty is. Great or small, splendid or obscure. Only to find our duty certainly, and somewhere, somehow, to do it faithfully, makes us good, strong, happy and useful men, and tunes our lives into some feeble echo of the life of God.

—*Phillips Brooks.*

HELPS TO HAPPINESS

Without distinction, without calculation, without procrastination, love. Lavish it upon the poor, where it is very easy; especially upon the rich, who often need it most; most of all upon our equals, where it is very difficult, and for whom perhaps we each do least of all.

—Henry Drummond.

HELPS TO HAPPINESS

It is not work that kills men; it is worry. Work is healthy; you can hardly put more upon a man than he can bear. Worry is rust upon the blade. It is not the revolution that destroys the machinery, but the friction.
—*Henry Ward Beecher.*

I think that good must come of good,
And ill of evil—surely unto all
In every place or time, seeing sweet fruit
Groweth from wholesome roots, or bitter things
From poison stocks: yea, seeing, too, how spite
Breeds hate—and kindness friends—or patience
Peace. —*Edwin Arnold.*

It is a wise man who knows his own business; and a wiser one who thoroughly attends to it. —*H. L. Wayland.*

"In the morning of life, work; in the midday, give counsel; in the evening, pray."

The very art of life, far as I have been able to observe, consists in fortitude and perseverance. —*Walter Scott.*

Our friends see the best in us, and by that very fact call forth the best from us.
—*Black.*

HELPS TO HAPPINESS

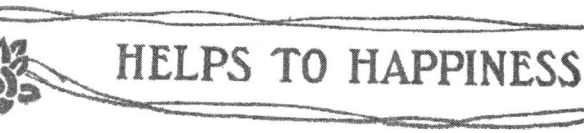

THE RECESSIONAL.

God of our fathers, known of old,
    Lord of our far-flung battle line,
Beneath whose awful hand we hold
    Dominion over palm and pine,
Lord God of Hosts, be with us yet,
Lest we forget—lest we forget!

The tumult and the shouting dies,
    The Captains and the Kings depart,
Still stands Thine ancient sacrifice,
    A humble and a contrite heart.
Lord God of Hosts, be with us yet,
Lest we forget—lest we forget!

Far-called, our navies melt away,
    On dune and headland sinks the fire,
Lo, all our pomp of yesterday
    Is one with Nineveh and Tyre!
Judge of the Nations, spare us yet,
Lest we forget—lest we forget!

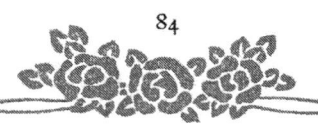

HELPS TO HAPPINESS

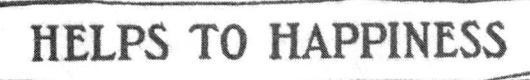

If, drunk with sight of power, we loose
    Wild tongues that have not Thee in awe,
Such boasting as the Gentiles use,
    Or lesser breeds without the Law,
Lord God of Hosts, be with us yet,
Lest we forget—lest we forget!

For heathen heart that puts her trust
    In reeking tube and iron shard,
All valiant dust that builds on dust,
    And guarding calls not Thee to guard,
For frantic boast and foolish word,
Thy Mercy on Thy People, Lord!
                    —Amen.
              —*Rudyard Kipling.*

HELPS TO HAPPINESS

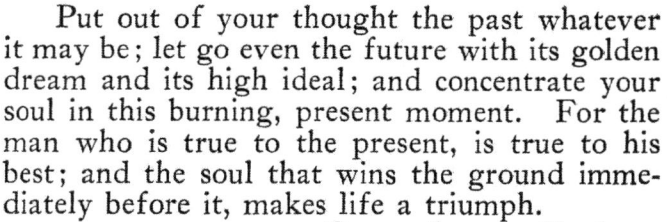

Put out of your thought the past whatever it may be; let go even the future with its golden dream and its high ideal; and concentrate your soul in this burning, present moment. For the man who is true to the present, is true to his best; and the soul that wins the ground immediately before it, makes life a triumph.
—*Ozora Stearns Davis.*

The most unhappy man or woman on earth is the one who rises in the morning with nothing to do and wonders how he will pass off the day.
—*Leslie M. Shaw.*

If to do were as easy as to know what were good to do, chapels had been churches, and poor men's cottages princes' palaces.
—*Shakespeare.*

It is easy to sit outside and say how the man inside should run the machine, but it is not so easy to go inside and run the machine yourself.
—*Theodore Roosevelt.*

You find yourself refreshed by the presence of cheerful people. Why not make earnest effort to confer that pleasure on others! You will find half the battle is gained if you never allow yourself to say anything gloomy.
—*L. M. Child.*

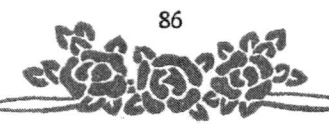

HELPS TO HAPPINESS

Rest is not idleness, and to lie sometimes on the grass under the trees on a summer's day, listening to the murmur of water, or watching the clouds float across the sky, is by no means waste of time. —*J. Lubbock.*

To-day is given us by Him to whom belong days—we have the power to use it as we please; we are responsible for its proper use; how important that we do the proper work of to-day in the sphere of to-day! —*Abraham Lincoln.*

It is hard to fail, but it is worse never to have tried to succeed. In this life we get nothing save by effort. —*Theodore Roosevelt.*

To live content with small means; to seek elegance rather than luxury, and refinement rather than fashion; to be worthy, not respectable and wealthy, not rich; to study hard, think quietly, talk gently, act frankly; to listen to stars and birds, to babes and sages, with open heart; to bear all cheerfully, do all bravely, await occasions, hurry never—in a word, to let the spiritual, unbidden and unconscious, grow up through the common: this is to be my symphony.
—*William Henry Channing.*

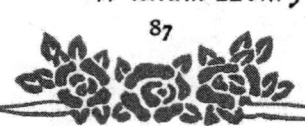

HELPS TO HAPPINESS

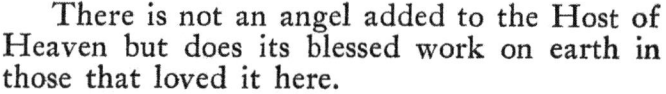

There is not an angel added to the Host of Heaven but does its blessed work on earth in those that loved it here.
—*Charles Dickens.*

The choir invisible! Who are members of it, if not all those who in any way are doing the day's work, whatever it may be, as well as they know how; who are trying to make the world happier and pleasanter for those to whom their lives are naturally bound.
—*John White Chadwick.*

Let us never covet fluency; it is a fatal gift. Let every man covet eloquence. It is to speak the right thing at the right time, in the right way.
—*F. W. Robertson.*

Let the weakest, let the humblest remember, that in his daily course he can, if he will, shed around him almost a heaven. Kindly words, sympathizing attentions, watchfulness against wounding men's sensitiveness—these cost very little, but they are priceless in their value. Are they not almost the staple of our daily happiness? From hour to hour, from moment to moment, we are supported, blest, by small kindnesses.
—*F. W. Robertson.*

HELPS TO HAPPINESS

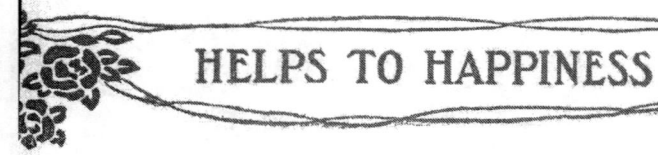

"Worship God by doing good,
  Works, not words; kind acts, not creeds!
He who loves God as he should
  Makes his heart's love understood by kind deeds."

HELPS TO HAPPINESS

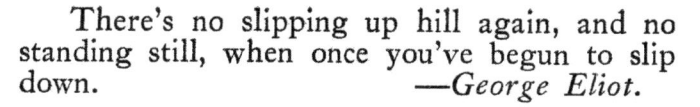

There's no slipping up hill again, and no standing still, when once you've begun to slip down. —*George Eliot.*

Prosperity is the blessing of the Old Testament; adversity is the blessing of the New.
Prosperity is not without many fears and distastes; and adversity is not without comforts and hopes. —*Bacon.*

And only the Master shall praise us,
  And only the Master shall blame,
And no one shall work for money,
  And no one shall work for fame:
But each for the joy of the working and each in his separate star
Shall draw the Thing as he sees it for the God of things as they are.
—*Rudyard Kipling.*

This life is a short minute. Eternity follows. —*Roger Williams.*

There are people who go about the world looking for slights and they are necessarily miserable, for they find them at every turn.
—*Henry Drummond.*

The business of life is largely made up of minute affairs, requiring only judgment and diligence. —*Henry Ward Beecher.*

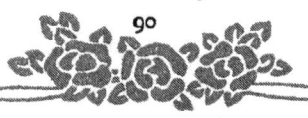

HELPS TO HAPPINESS

We have need of patience with ourselves and with others; with those below, and those above us, and with our own equals; with those who love us and those who love us not; for the greatest things and for the least; against sudden inroads of trouble, and under our daily burdens; disappointments as to the weather; or the breaking of the heart; in the weariness of the body, or the wearing of the soul; in our own failure of duty, or others' failure toward us; in everyday wants, or in the aching of sickness or the decay of age; in disappointment, bereavement, losses, injuries, reproaches; in heaviness of the heart, or its sickness amid delayed hopes. In all these things, from childhood's little troubles to the martyr's sufferings, patience is the grace of God, whereby we endure evil for the love of God. —*E. B. Pusey.*

HELPS TO HAPPINESS

Let men see that you are real—inconsistent, it may be—sinful, oh! full of sin, impetuous, hasty, perhaps stern. But compel them to feel that you are earnest. This is the secret of influence. —*F. W. Robertson.*

A great part of the happiness of life consists not in fighting battles, but in avoiding them. A masterly retreat is in itself a victory.
—*Longfellow.*

Industry is one other really great thing you will need. If you want the highest positions you must pay the price. This world runs a one-priced store and has no bargain-counter. Don't expect the goods unless you pay the price. You may have to burn midnight oil and work while others sleep, but that's the price. You don't have to pay it, but that's the price if you want the goods. —*Leslie M. Shaw.*

HELPS TO HAPPINESS

Young men, you are the architects of your own fortunes. Rely upon your own strength of body and soul. Take for your star, self-reliance. Don't take too much advice—keep at your helm and steer your own ship, and remember that the great art of commanding is to take a fair share of the work. Think well of yourself. Strike out. Be in earnest. Be self-reliant. Be generous. Be civil. Read the papers. Advertise your business. Make money, and do good with it. Love your God and fellow-men. Love truth and virtue. Love your country and obey its laws. —*Porter.*

HELPS TO HAPPINESS

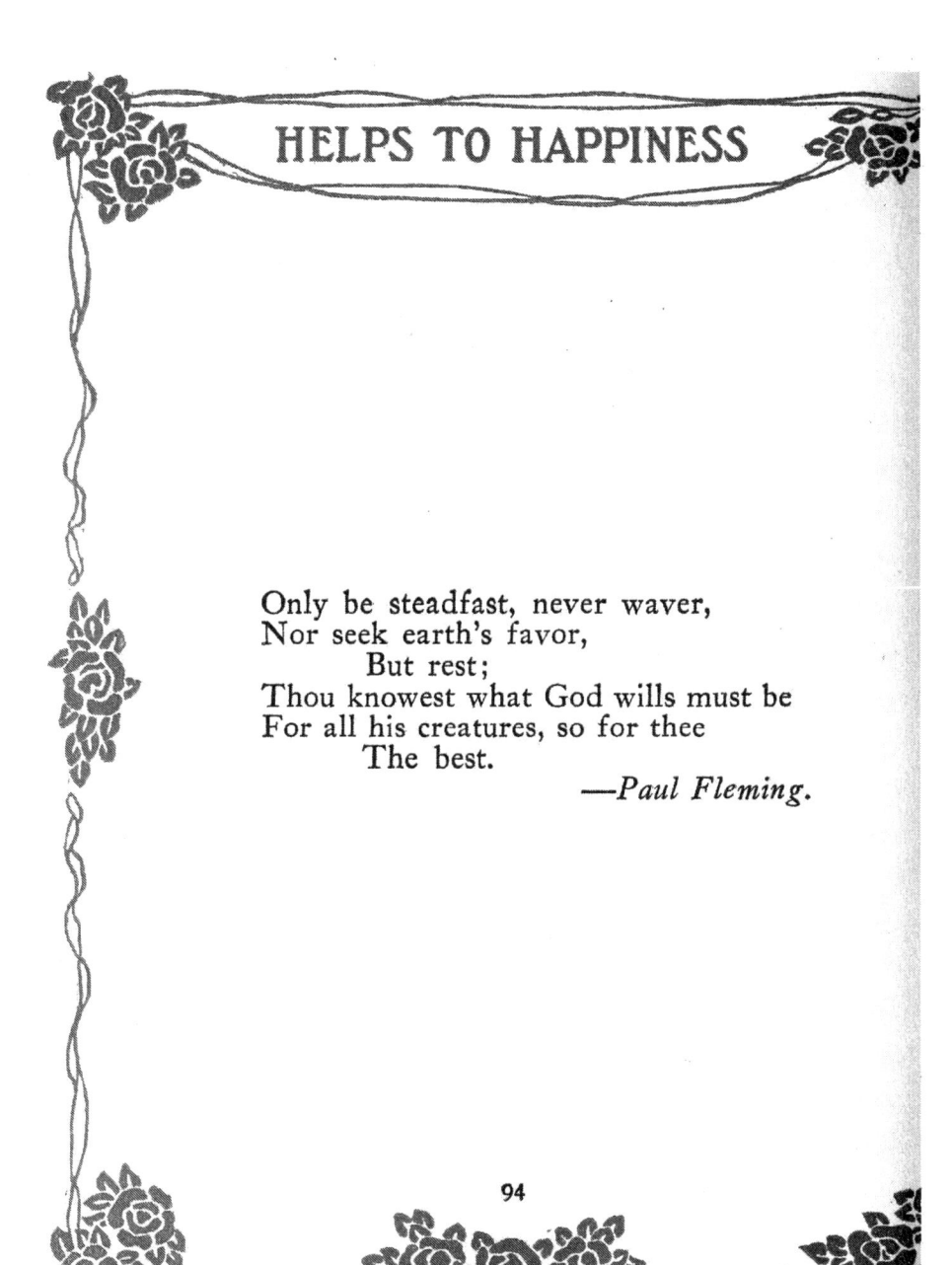

Only be steadfast, never waver,
Nor seek earth's favor,
    But rest;
Thou knowest what God wills must be
For all his creatures, so for thee
    The best.

—Paul Fleming.

HELPS TO HAPPINESS

Wherever souls are being tried and ripened, in whatever commonplace and homely way, there God is hewing out pillars for his temple.
—*Phillips Brooks.*

It is by doing our duty that we learn to do it. So long as men dispute whether or no a thing is their duty, they get never the nearer. Let them set ever so weakly about doing it, and the face of things alters. They find in themselves strength which they knew not of.
—*E. B. Pusey.*

If we want light, we must conquer darkness.
—*J. T. Fields.*

Seek your life's nourishment in your life's work.
—*Phillips Brooks.*

If there be no nobility of descent, all the more indispensable is it that there should be nobility of ascent,—a character in them that bear rule so fine and high and pure that as men come within the circle of its influence they involuntarily pay homage to that which is the one preeminent distinction, the royalty of virtue.
—*Henry C. Potter.*

HELPS TO HAPPINESS

Consider the postage stamp, my son. It secures success through its ability to stick to one thing till it gets there. —*Josh Billings*.

"Of all the lights you carry in your face, joy shines farthest out to sea."

The test of your Christian character should be that you are a joy-bearing agent to the world.
—*Henry Ward Beecher*.

Just to fill the hour—that is happiness.
—*Emerson*.

God is as willing that you should read your lesson in the sunlight as in the storm.
—*Phillips Brooks*.

What stronger breastplate than a heart untainted?
Thrice is he armed that hath his quarrel just;
And he but naked, though locked up in steel,
Whose conscience with injustice is corrupted.
—*Shakespeare*.

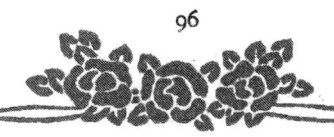

HELPS TO HAPPINESS

A ruddy drop of manly blood
    The surging sea outweighs,
The world uncertain comes and goes;
    The lover rooted stays.

I fancied he was fled—
    And, after many a year,
Glowed unexhausted kindliness,
    Like daily sunrise there.

My careful heart was free again,
    O friend, my bosom said,
Through thee alone the sky is arched,
    Through thee the rose is red.

Me too thy nobleness has taught
    To master my despair;
The fountains of my hidden life
    Are through thy friendship fair.
                  —*Emerson.*

HELPS TO HAPPINESS

Speak softly and carry a big stick—you will go far. —*Theodore Roosevelt.*

How many simple ways there are to bless.
—*Lowell.*

Our country calls not for the life of ease, but for the life of strenuous endeavor.
—*Theodore Roosevelt.*

But evil is wrought by want of thought,
As well as want of heart.
—*Thomas Hood.*

Men are four:
He who knows, and knows he knows,—
 He is wise—follow him.
He who knows, and knows not he knows,—
 He is asleep—wake him:—
He who knows not, and knows not he knows not,—
 He is a fool—shun him.
He who knows not, and knows he knows not,—
 He is a child—teach him.
—*Arabian Proverb.*

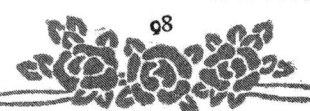

HELPS TO HAPPINESS

For right is right, since God is God,
    And right the day must win;
To doubt would be disloyalty,
    To falter would be sin.
                     —*F. W. Faber.*

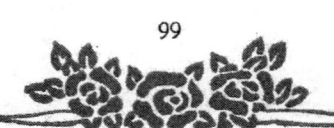

HELPS TO HAPPINESS

"When a man leaves our side and goes to the other side he is a traitor. But when a man leaves the other side and comes over to us, then he is a man of great moral courage, and we always felt that he had sterling stuff in him."

Good deeds ring clear through heaven like a bell.
—Charles Dickens.

A waistcoat of broadcloth or of fustian is alike to an aching heart, and we laugh no merrier on velvet cushions than we did on wooden chairs.
—J. K. Jerome.

No one is so accursed by fate,
No one so utterly desolate,
But some heart, though unknown,
Responds unto his own.
—Longfellow.

It is better to go down on the great seas which human hearts were made to sail than to rot at the wharves in ignoble anchorage.
—Hamilton W. Mabie.

HELPS TO HAPPINESS

"When in doubt, tell the truth."

How hard it is to confess that we have spoken without thinking, that we have talked nonsense! How many a man says a thing in haste or in heat, without fully understanding or half meaning it, and then, because he has said it, holds fast to it, and tries to defend it as if it were true! But how much wiser, how much more admirable and attractive, it is when a man has the grace to perceive and acknowledge his mistakes! It gives us assurance that he is capable of learning, of growing, of improving so that his future will be better than his past.

Truth forever on the scaffold; Wrong forever
    on the throne;
Yet that scaffold sways the future and beyond
    the dim unknown
Standeth God within the shadow, keeping watch
    above his own.
—*Lowell.*

"A tree is known by its fruit and not by its leaves."

We should be as careful of our words as of our actions, and as far from speaking ill as from doing ill. —*Cicero.*

HELPS TO HAPPINESS

Perseverance is irresistible.
—*Sertorius.*

Thank God every morning when you get up that you have something to do that day, which must be done whether you like it or not. Being forced to work, and forced to do your best, will breed in you . . . a hundred virtues which the idle never know. —*Charles Kingsley.*

Nothing is ever done beautifully, which is done in rivalship; nor nobly, which is done in pride. —*Ruskin.*

The first test of a truly great man is his humility. All great men not only know their business, but usually know that they know it, and are not only right in their main opinions but usually know that they are right in them; only they do not think much of themselves on that account and they see something divine in every other man. —*Ruskin.*

HELPS TO HAPPINESS

If you and I—just you and I—
  Should laugh instead of worry;
If we should grow—just you and I—
  Kinder and sweeter hearted,
Perhaps in some near by and by
  A good time might get started;
Then what a happy world 'twould be
  For you and me—for you and me!

HELPS TO HAPPINESS

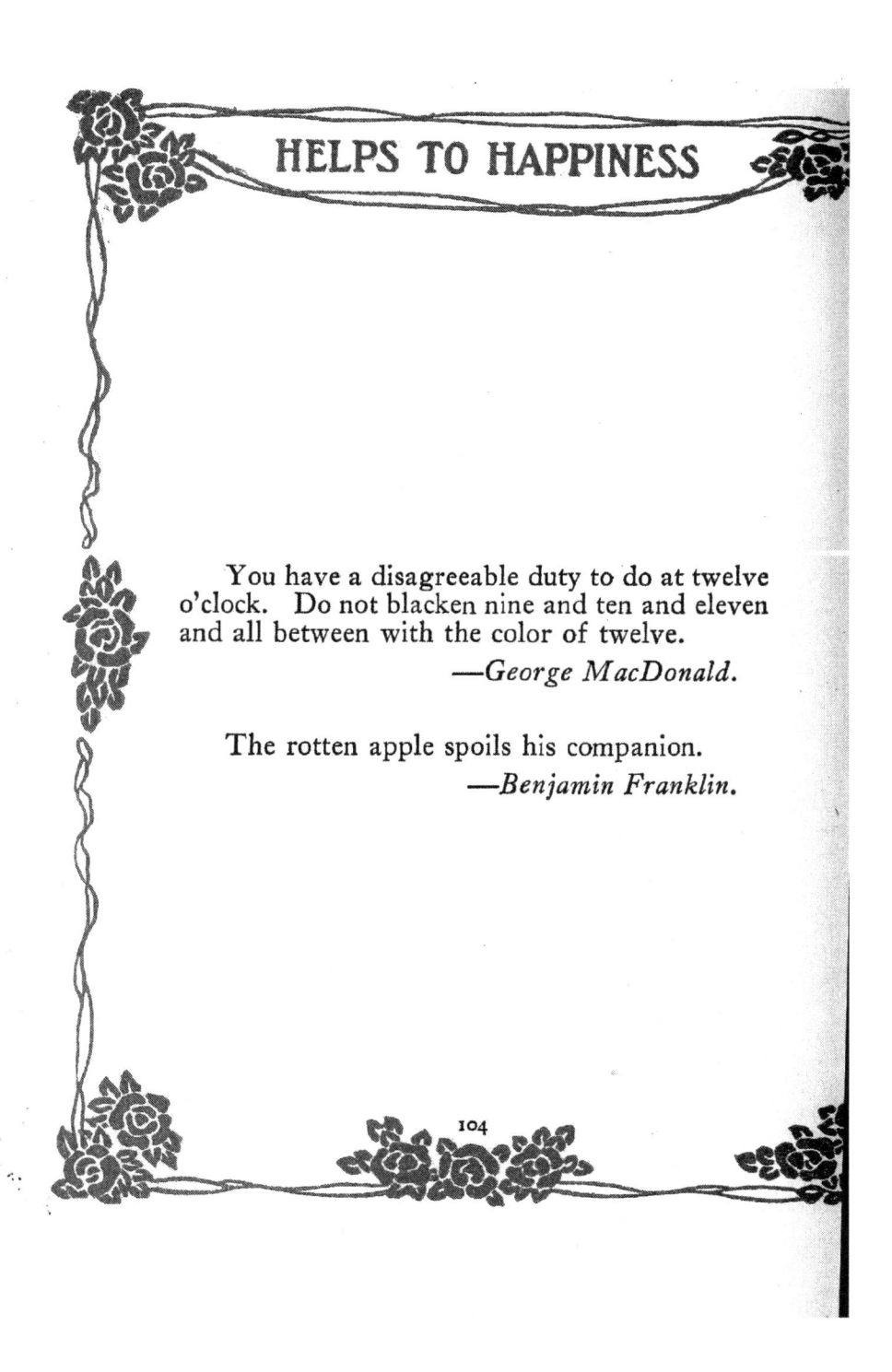

You have a disagreeable duty to do at twelve o'clock. Do not blacken nine and ten and eleven and all between with the color of twelve.
—*George MacDonald.*

The rotten apple spoils his companion.
—*Benjamin Franklin.*

HELPS TO HAPPINESS

I find earth not gray, but rosy,
   Heaven not grim, but fair of hue.
Do I stoop? I pick a posy;
   Do I stand and stare? All's blue.
—*Robert Browning.*

"A thankful heart is not only the greatest virtue, but the parent of all the other virtues."

Wise men ne'er sit and wail their loss,
But cheerily seek how to redress their harms.
What though the mast be now blown overboard,
The cable broke, the holding anchor lost,
And half our sailors swallowed in the flood—
Yet lives our Pilot still.   —*Shakespeare.*

"Happiness does not depend on money or leisure, or society, or even on health; it depends on our relation to those we love."

I am quite sure that one secret of youth is to keep up with determined and steady hand, one's own tone, to avoid ruts and narrowing circles. —*J. F. W. Ware.*

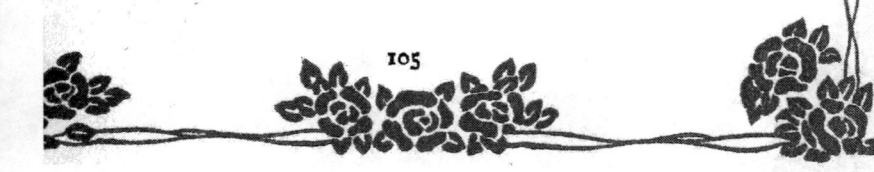

HELPS TO HAPPINESS

Never esteem anything as of advantage to thee that shall make thee break thy word or lose thy self-respect. —*Marcus Aurelius.*

Take hold, my son, of the toughest knots worthy of man's highest estate; have high, noble, manly honor. There is but one test of everything, and that is, is it right? If it is not, turn right away from it. —*Henry A. Wise.*

A happy man or woman is a better thing to find than a five pound note. The entrance of such a person into a room is as if another candle had been lighted.
—*Robert Louis Stevenson.*

The way to do a thing is to go and do it. If there is a particularly disagreeable task before you, begin with that, and so save yourself several hours of dread, aside from having it done the sooner. —*Swett.*

Let us be content, in work, to do the thing we *can* and not presume to fret because it's little.
—*Elizabeth Barrett Browning.*

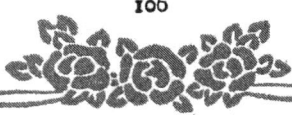

HELPS TO HAPPINESS

OH how hard it is to die and not be able to leave the world any better for one's little life in it!

Abraham Lincoln.

HELPS TO HAPPINESS

We must not take the faults of our youth into our old age; for old age brings with it its own faults. —*Goethe.*

Neglect of small things is the rock on which the great majority of the human race have split.
—*Samuel Smiles.*

It is only by thinking about great and good things that we come to love them, and it is only by loving them that we come to long for them, and it is only by longing for them that we are impelled to seek after them, and it is only by seeking after them that they become ours and we enter into vital experience of their beauty and blessedness. —*Henry van Dyke.*

A great deal of discomfort arises from over-sensitiveness about what people may say of you or your actions. Many unhappy persons seem to imagine that they are always in an amphitheatre, with the assembled world as spectators; whereas, all the while, they are playing to empty benches. —*Arthur Helps.*

HELPS TO HAPPINESS

*HOW DID YOU DIE?

Did you tackle that trouble that came your way
   With a resolute heart and cheerful?
Or hide your face from the light of day
   With a craven soul and fearful?
Oh, a trouble's a ton, or a trouble's an ounce,
   Or a trouble is what you make it,
And it isn't the fact that you're hurt that counts,
   But only how did you take it?
—Edmund Vance Cooke.

*From "Impertinent Poems"

Then a voice within his breast
   Whispered, audible and clear:
"Do thy duty; that is best;
   Leave unto the Lord the rest!"
—Longfellow.

HELPS TO HAPPINESS

Every duty we omit obscures some truth we should have known.
—*Ruskin.*

O day of rest! How beautiful, how fair,
How welcome to the weary and the old!
Day of the Lord! and truce to earthly care!
Day of the Lord, as all our days should be.
—*Longfellow.*

The more you say, the less people remember. The fewer the words, the greater the profit.
—*Fenelon.*

Let all your things have their places; let each part of your business have its time. Resolve to perform what you ought; perform, without fail, what you resolve. Lose no time! Be always employed in something useful.
—*Benjamin Franklin.*

The greatest of faults, I should say, is to be conscious of none. —*Thomas Carlyle.*

Nine-tenths of the miseries and vices of mankind proceed from idleness.
—*Thomas Carlyle.*

HELPS TO HAPPINESS

Men give me credit for genius; but all the genius I have lies in this: When I have a subject on hand I study it profoundly. The effect I make, they call the fruit of genius; it is, however, the fruit of labor and thought.
—*Alexander Hamilton.*

Be the noblest man that your present faith, poor and weak and imperfect as it is, can make you be. Live up to your present growth, your present faith. So, and so only, do you take the next straight step forward, as you stand strong where you are now; so only can you think the curtain will be drawn back and there will be revealed to you what lies beyond.
—*Phillips Brooks.*

"Folded hands are ever weary,
  Selfish hearts are never gay;
Life for thee hath many duties,
  Active be, then, while you may."
  Be strong to hope, O Heart!
    Though day is bright,
  The stars can only shine
    In the dark night.
  Be strong, O heart of mine;
    Look towards the light.
—*A. Procter.*

HELPS TO HAPPINESS

Every duty we omit obscures some truth we should have known. —*Ruskin.*

O day of rest! How beautiful, how fair,
How welcome to the weary and the old!
Day of the Lord! and truce to earthly care!
Day of the Lord, as all our days should be.
—*Longfellow.*

The more you say, the less people remember. The fewer the words, the greater the profit.
—*Fenelon.*

Let all your things have their places; let each part of your business have its time. Resolve to perform what you ought; perform, without fail, what you resolve. Lose no time! Be always employed in something useful.
—*Benjamin Franklin.*

The greatest of faults, I should say, is to be conscious of none. —*Thomas Carlyle.*

Nine-tenths of the miseries and vices of mankind proceed from idleness.
—*Thomas Carlyle.*

HELPS TO HAPPINESS

Men give me credit for genius; but all the genius I have lies in this: When I have a subject on hand I study it profoundly. The effect I make, they call the fruit of genius; it is, however, the fruit of labor and thought.
—*Alexander Hamilton.*

Be the noblest man that your present faith, poor and weak and imperfect as it is, can make you be. Live up to your present growth, your present faith. So, and so only, do you take the next straight step forward, as you stand strong where you are now; so only can you think the curtain will be drawn back and there will be revealed to you what lies beyond.
—*Phillips Brooks.*

"Folded hands are ever weary,
  Selfish hearts are never gay;
Life for thee hath many duties,
  Active be, then, while you may."
  Be strong to hope, O Heart!
    Though day is bright,
  The stars can only shine
    In the dark night.
  Be strong, O heart of mine;
    Look towards the light.
—*A. Procter.*

HELPS TO HAPPINESS

MY PRAYER.

If there be some weaker one,
Give me strength to help him on;
If a blinder soul there be,
Let me guide him nearer thee,
Make my mortal dreams come true
With the work I fain would do;
Clothe with life the weak intent,
Let me be the thing I meant;
Let me find in thy employ
Peace that dearer is than joy;
Out of self to love be led,
And to heaven acclimated,
Until all things sweet and good
Seem my nature's habitude.
—*John G. Whittier.*

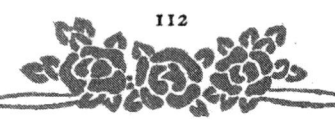

HELPS TO HAPPINESS

Let us have faith that right makes might; and in that faith let us, to the end, dare to do our duty, as we understand it.
—*Abraham Lincoln.*

He who is false to present duty breaks a thread in the loom, and will find the flaw when he may have forgotten its cause.
—*Henry Ward Beecher.*

If money be not thy servant, it will be thy master. The covetous man can not so properly be said to possess wealth, as that may be said to possess him. —*Bacon.*

"Choose a book as you would choose a friend."

Be sure you give me the best of your wares, though they be poor enough; and the gods will help you to lay by a better store for the future.
—*Henry David Thoreau.*

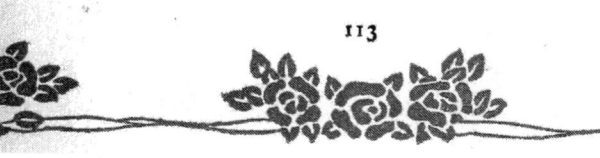

HELPS TO HAPPINESS

The heights by great men reached and kept,
   Were not attained by sudden flight;
But they, while their companions slept,
   Were toiling upward in the night.
—*Longfellow.*

Seek not to have things happen as you choose them, but rather choose them to happen as they do, and so shall you live prosperously.
—*Epictetus.*

Whatever the number of a man's friends, there will be times in his life when he has one too few; but if he has only one enemy, he is lucky indeed, if he has not one too many.
—*Bulwer.*

It is not for nothing that a man has in him sympathies with some principles and repugnance to others. He, with all his capacities, and aspirations, and beliefs, is not an accident, but a product of the time. * * * The highest truth he sees the wise man will fearlessly utter; knowing that, let what may come of it, he is thus playing his right part in the world.
—*Herbert Spencer.*

HELPS TO HAPPINESS

Are you in earnest? Seize this very minute,
What you can do, or dream you can, begin it;
Boldness has genius, power and magic in it.
Only engage and then the mind grows heated;
Begin and then the work will be completed.
—*Goethe.*

HELPS TO HAPPINESS

Free men freely work. Whoever fears God fears to sit at ease.
—*Elizabeth Barrett Browning.*

"Taking trouble is the best way of avoiding troubles. The lack of taking trouble has been the means of making trouble in many lives."

As a tired mother when the day is o'er,
   Leads by the hand her little child to bed,
   Half willing, half reluctant to be led,
And leaves his broken playthings on the floor,
Still gazing at them through the open door,
   Nor wholly reassured and comforted
   By promises of others in their stead,
Which, though more splendid, may not please him more;
So Nature deals with us and takes away
   Our playthings one by one, and by the hand
   Leads us to rest so gently that we go
Scarce knowing if we wish to go or stay,
   Being too full of sleep to understand
     How far the unknown transcends the what we know.   —*Longfellow.*

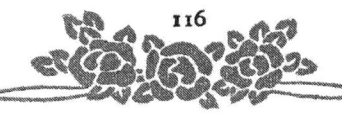

HELPS TO HAPPINESS

A little work, a little play
To keep us going—and so, good-day!
A little warmth, a little light
Of love's bestowing—and so, good-night!
A little fun to match the sorrow
Of each day's growing—and so, good-morrow!
A little trust that when we die
We reap our sowing! And so—good-bye!
—*George Du Maurier.*

What makes life dreary is want of motive.
—*George Eliot.*

O do not pray for easy lives. Pray to be stronger men. Do not pray for tasks equal to your powers. Pray for powers equal to your tasks. Then the doing of your work shall be no miracle. But you shall be a miracle. Every day you shall wonder at yourself, at the richness of life which has come to you by the grace of God.
—*Phillips Brooks.*

HELPS TO HAPPINESS

Every hand is wanted in this world that can do a little genuine, sincere work.
—*George Eliot.*

Go, put your creed into your deed,
   Nor speak with double tongue.
—*Emerson.*

"The man who won the hurdle race,
   I'll mention here, my son,
That he never would have won it
   If he hadn't tried to run.
The man who did the splendid thing,
   As all of us now grant,
He never would have done it
   Had he stopped to say, 'I can't.' "

Cast forth thy act, thy word, into the ever-living, ever-working universe; it is a seed-grain that cannot die.
—*Thomas Carlyle.*

Better a day of strife
Than a century of sleep.
—*Father Ryan.*

HELPS TO HAPPINESS

There are more opportunities than there are young men to take advantage of them. You say the country has grown larger, that life is more complex and that as a result the personal incentive has vanished in proportion. Everything in that is perfectly correct except the conclusion. The country is bigger and life is more complex, but who will gainsay that if the country has grown bigger and the opportunities have with it, and that if life is more complex, it at least results in a greater variety of opportunities.

—*James J. Hill.*

HELPS TO HAPPINESS

If I knew you and you knew me; if both of us could clearly see,
And with an inner sight divine the meaning of your heart and mine,
I'm sure that we would differ less and clasp our hands in friendliness,
Our thoughts would pleasantly agree if I knew you and you knew me.
—*Nixon Waterman.*

We all have to learn, in one way or another, that neither men nor boys get *second* chances in this world. We all get *new* chances to the end of our lives, but not second chances in the same set of circumstances; and the great difference between one person and another is how he takes hold and uses his first chance, and how he takes his fall if it is scored against him.

—*Thomas Hughes.*

There is positive proof in the single sunbeam of the existence of the sun.
—*Phillips Brooks.*

HELPS TO HAPPINESS

Stay, stay at home, my heart, and rest;
Home-keeping hearts are happiest;
For they that wander, they know not where,
Are full of trouble, and full of care;
To stay at home is best. —*Longfellow.*

HELPS TO HAPPINESS

We make provisions for this life as if it were never to have an end, and for the other life as though it were never to have a beginning.
—*Addison.*

The surest way not to fail is to determine to succeed. —*Sheridan.*

There is genius and power in persistence. It conquers all opposers; it gives confidence; it annihilates obstacles. Everybody believes in the determined man. People know that when he undertakes a thing, the battle is half won, for his rule is to accomplish whatever he sets out to do. People know that it is useless to oppose a man who uses his stumbling blocks as stepping stones; who does not know when he is defeated; who never, because of criticism or opposition, shrinks from his task. —*Orison Swett Marden.*

Knowledge and timber shouldn't be much used till they are seasoned. —*Holmes.*

HELPS TO HAPPINESS

Here, in this little Bay,
  Full of tumultuous life and great repose,
Where, twice a day,
  The purposeless, glad ocean comes and goes,
Under high cliffs, and far from the huge town,
I sit me down.
For want of me the world's course will not fail;
  When all its work is done the lies shall rot;
The truth is great and shall prevail,
  When none cares whether it prevail or not.
—*Coventry Patmore.*

"The habit of helplessness begins early. It grows and with many men becomes fixed before the voting age. The first symptom is the dodging of responsibility, the effort to unload on to somebody else."

The essential tendency of life is towards happiness . . . Optimism is the only true condition for a reasonable man.
—*Phillips Brooks.*

The reason I beat the Austrians is, they did not know the value of five minutes.
—*Napoleon I.*

HELPS TO HAPPINESS

Hearts only thrive on varied good;
   And he who gathers from a host
Of friendly hearts his daily food,
   Is the best friend that we can boast.
—J. G. Holland.

There are two good rules which ought to be written on every heart: Never believe anything bad about anybody unless you positively know it is true; never tell even that, unless you feel that it is absolutely necessary, and that God is listening while you tell it.
—Henry van Dyke.

I am glad to think
I am not bound to make the wrong go right,
But only to discover and to do,
With cheerful heart, the work that God appoints.
—Jean Ingelow.

If you want to be miserable, think about yourself, about what you want, what you like, what respect people ought to pay you, and what people think of you. *—Charles Kingsley.*

HELPS TO HAPPINESS

Insist on yourself; never imitate. There is at this moment for you an utterance brave and grand as that of the colossal chisel of Phidias, or the pen of Moses or Dante, but different from these. If you can hear what these patriarchs say, surely you can reply to them in the same pitch of voice.
—*Emerson.*

*FAILURE.

What is a failure? It's only a spur
　To a man who receives it right,
And it makes the spirit within him stir
　To go in once more and fight.
If you never have failed it's an even guess,
You never have won a high success.
—*Edmund Vance Cooke.*

*From "Impertinent Poems"

But noble souls through dust and heat
Rise from disaster and defeat
　　The stronger.
—*Longfellow.*

"Opportunity does not force itself upon us. If we are not watching it slips by and we lose it forever."

HELPS TO HAPPINESS

Be of good cheer, brave spirit; steadfastly serve that low whisper thou hast served; for know, God hath a select family of sons now scattered wide thro' earth, and each alone, who are thy spiritual kindred, and each one by constant service to that inward law, is weaving the sublime proportions of a true monarch's soul. Beauty and strength, the riches of a spotless memory, the eloquence of truth, the wisdom got by searching of a clear and loving eye that seeth as God seeth. These are their gifts, and Time, who keeps God's word, brings on the day to seal the marriage of these minds with thine, thine everlasting lovers. Ye shall be the salt of all the elements, world of the world.

—Emerson.

HELPS TO HAPPINESS

The secret of success lies not in doing your own work, but in recognizing the right man to do it.
—*Andrew Carnegie.*

It is astonishing what a lot of odd minutes one can catch during the day, if one really sets about it.
—*Dinah Maria Mulock.*

Energy, system, perseverence—these are the great components of success in a young man's life, and with them he is bound to succeed as well to-day as he ever succeeded. He must have a set standard of achievement; he must make up his mind what he is going to do in the world and then keep fighting for this standard.
—*James J. Hill.*

"The secret of success consists not in the habit of making numerous resolutions about various faults and sins, but in one great, absorbing, controlling purpose to serve God and do His will! If this be the controlling motive of life, all other motives will be swept into the force of its mighty current and guided aright."

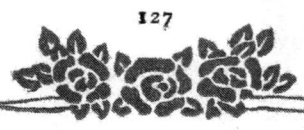

HELPS TO HAPPINESS

For what doth the Lord require of thee, but to do justly, and to love mercy, and to walk humbly with thy God?
—*Micah.*

No man need hunt for his mission. His mission comes to him. It is not above, it is not below, it is not far—not to make happy human faces now and then among the children of misery, but to keep happy human faces about us all the time.
—*J. F. W. Ware.*

Every life is meant
To help all lives; each man should live
For all men's betterment.
—*Alice Cary.*

For a man to *grow* a gentleman, it is of great consequence that his grandfather should have been an honest man; but if a man *be* a gentleman, it matters little what his grandfather, or grandmother either, was.
—*George MacDonald.*

Where the press is free, and every man able to read, all is safe.
—*Thomas Jefferson.*

HELPS TO HAPPINESS

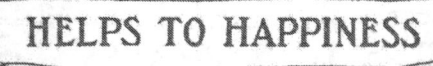

The first hour of the morning is the rudder of the day.
—*Henry Ward Beecher.*

Life is not so short but that there is always time enough for courtesy.
—*Emerson.*

We need, each and all, to be needed,
   To feel we have something to give
Towards soothing the moan of earth's hunger
   And we know that then only we live
When we feed one another as we have been fed,
From the hand that gives body and spirit their
      bread.
—*Lucy Larcom.*

"The true optimists of life are not those who have always 'had things easy,' and know nothing of care or trouble; neither are they the ones who resolutely refuse to acknowledge the presence of sin and sorrow. They are those who determine to meet facts honestly and can give themselves eagerly, untiringly, to fighting the sin and lessening the sorrow and the pain."

HELPS TO HAPPINESS

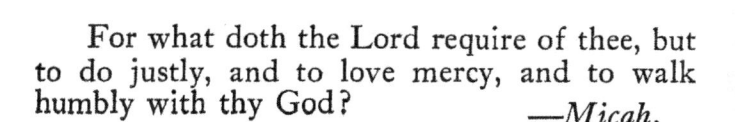

For what doth the Lord require of thee, but to do justly, and to love mercy, and to walk humbly with thy God?
—*Micah.*

No man need hunt for his mission. His mission comes to him. It is not above, it is not below, it is not far—not to make happy human faces now and then among the children of misery, but to keep happy human faces about us all the time.
—*J. F. W. Ware.*

Every life is meant
To help all lives; each man should live
For all men's betterment.
—*Alice Cary.*

For a man to *grow* a gentleman, it is of great consequence that his grandfather should have been an honest man; but if a man *be* a gentleman, it matters little what his grandfather, or grandmother either, was.
—*George MacDonald.*

Where the press is free, and every man able to read, all is safe. —*Thomas Jefferson.*

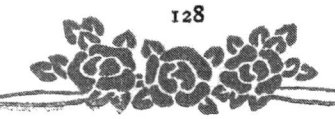

HELPS TO HAPPINESS

The first hour of the morning is the rudder of the day.
>—*Henry Ward Beecher.*

Life is not so short but that there is always time enough for courtesy.
>—*Emerson.*

We need, each and all, to be needed,
  To feel we have something to give
Towards soothing the moan of earth's hunger
  And we know that then only we live
When we feed one another as we have been fed,
From the hand that gives body and spirit their bread.
>—*Lucy Larcom.*

"The true optimists of life are not those who have always 'had things easy,' and know nothing of care or trouble; neither are they the ones who resolutely refuse to acknowledge the presence of sin and sorrow. They are those who determine to meet facts honestly and can give themselves eagerly, untiringly, to fighting the sin and lessening the sorrow and the pain."

HELPS TO HAPPINESS

The grand essentials of happiness are, something to do, something to love, and something to hope for.
—Chalmers.

It is not what a man gets, but what a man is, that he should think of. He should first think of his character, and then of his condition. He that has character need have no fears about his condition. Character will draw after it condition.
—Henry Ward Beecher.

HELPS TO HAPPINESS

Aim at perfection in everything though in most things it is unattainable However they who aim at it and persevere will come much nearer to it than those whose laziness and despondency make them give it up as unattainable

Chesterfield

HELPS TO HAPPINESS

The making of friends, who are real friends, is the best token we have of a man's success in life.
—*Edward Everett Hale.*

HELPS TO HAPPINESS

"Dreams fade, deeds fail and days depart—
And all is changed in time and place;—
Thrice blessed are the pure in heart
For only they shall see God's face."

Where there is Faith there is Love;
Where there is Love there is Peace;
Where there is Peace there is God;
Where there is God there is no Need.

"If you wish to be held in esteem you must associate only with those who are estimable."

The man who has begun to live more seriously within begins to live more simply without.
— *Phillips Brooks.*

The heart of man seeks for sympathy, and each of us craves a recognition of his talents and his labors. But this craving is in danger of becoming morbid, unless it be constantly kept in check by calm reflection on its vanity, or by dwelling upon the very different and far higher motives which should actuate us.
— *Arthur Helps.*

HELPS TO HAPPINESS

A man is simple when his chief care is the wish to be what he ought to be; that is, honestly and naturally human. We may compare existence to raw material. What it is, matters less than what is made of it; as the value of a work of art lies in the flowering of a workman's skill. True life is possible in social conditions in the most diverse, and with natural gifts the most unequal. It is not fortune, or personal advantage, but our turning them to account, that constitutes the value of life. Fame adds no more than does length of days; quality is the thing.

—*Charles Wagner.*

"Avoid multiplicity of business; the man of one thing is the man of success."

The strength of your life is measured by the strength of your will. But the strength of your will is just the strength of the wish that lies behind it. And the strength of your wish depends upon the sincerity and earnestness and tenacity with which you fix your attention upon the things which are really great and worthy to be loved.

—*Henry van Dyke.*

HELPS TO HAPPINESS

Do to-day thy nearest duty.
—*Goethe.*

HELPS TO HAPPINESS

A cottage will hold as much happiness as would stock a palace. —*James Hamilton.*

He travelled here, he travelled there;
But not the value of a hair
   Was head or heart the better.
—*Wordsworth.*

It is only a poor sort of happiness that could ever come by caring very much about our own narrow pleasures. We can only have the highest happiness by having wide thoughts, and much feeling for the rest of the world, as well as ourselves; and this sort of happiness often brings so much pain with it that we can only tell it from pain by its being what we would choose before everything else, because our souls see it is good.
—*George Eliot.*

The path of success in business is invariably the path of common sense. —*Samuel Smiles.*

HELPS TO HAPPINESS

Men have certain work to do for their bread, and that is to be done strenuously; other work for their delight, and that is to be done heartily; neither is to be done by halves or shifts, but with a will, and what is not worth that effort is not to be done at all. —*Ruskin.*

If we work upon marble, it will perish; if we work upon brass, time will efface it; if we rear temples, they will crumble into dust; but if we work upon immortal souls, if we imbue them with principles, with the just fear of God and love of fellow men, we engrave on those tablets something which will brighten all eternity. —*Daniel Webster.*

Remember this—that very little is needed to make a happy life. —*Marcus Aurelius.*

To-morrow, when you go into your business and find twenty thousand dollars that can easily be scooped up, and the law on your side—and the devil, too—look into the invisible and see the crown which angels have for him who shall say, "Get thee behind me, Satan."
—*Henry Ward Beecher.*

HELPS TO HAPPINESS

I hope I shall always possess firmness and virtue enough to maintain what I consider the most enviable of all titles, the character of an "honest man."
—*George Washington.*

The grand essentials of happiness are something to do, something to love, and something to hope for.
—*Chalmers.*

I know of no more encouraging fact than the unquestionable ability of a man to elevate his life by a conscious endeavor. It is something to be able to paint a particular picture, or to carve a statue, and so make a few objects beautiful; but it is far more glorious to carve and paint the very atmosphere and medium through which we look, which morally we can do.

—*Henry David Thoreau.*

Life is the highest gift that we have received. That gift should not be wasted. It must be made to serve the purpose which animated the mind of the Lord of Life when He gave it to us.
—*Charles Wagner.*

HELPS TO HAPPINESS

You will find as you look back upon your life that the moments that stand out, the moments when you have really lived, are the moments when you have done things in a spirit of love.   —*Henry Drummond.*

The man who has the good-will and the good-nature of the men among whom he lives, of the society in which he dwells, is like a craft that has wind and currents both in its favor.
  —*Henry Ward Beecher.*

Half the world is on the wrong scent in the pursuit of happiness. They think it consists in having and getting, and in being served by others. It consists in giving and in serving others.   —*Henry Drummond.*

If for the age to come, this hour
Of trial hath vicarious power,
And blessed by Thee, our present pain
Be Liberty's eternal gain;
 Thy will be done.
  —*John G. Whittier.*

HELPS TO HAPPINESS

If the day and the night are such that you greet them with joy, and life emits a fragrance like flowers and sweet-scented herbs, is more starry, more immortal,—that is your success. All nature is your congratulation and you have cause momentarily to bless yourself.

—*Henry David Thoreau.*

In deciding a matter of importance bring yourself to the point by such questions as these: What has been done? What is the state of the case at present? What ought to be done? Express in writing the answers to your questions.

—*Arthur Helps.*

One never speaks of himself except at a loss.
—*Montaigne.*

Pin thy faith to no man's sleeve; hast thou not two eyes of thine own?

—*Thomas Carlyle.*

There is only one way to get ready for immortality, and that is to love this life, and live it as bravely and faithfully and cheerfully as we can.
—*Henry van Dyke.*

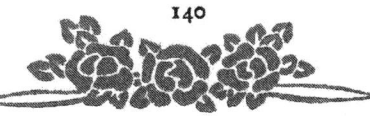

HELPS TO HAPPINESS

If you want to succeed in the world you must make your own opportunities as you go on. The man who waits for some seventh wave to toss him on dry land will find that the seventh wave is a long time coming. You can commit no greater folly than to sit by the roadside until some one comes along and invites you to ride with him to wealth or influence.

—*John B. Gough.*

HELPS TO HAPPINESS

Every thought and word and deed, of every human being, is followed by its inevitable consequence: for the one we are responsible; with the other we have nothing to do.
—*Gail Hamilton.*

Our grand business undoubtedly is: Not to seek for that which lies dimly in the future, but to do that which lies clearly at hand.
—*Thomas Carlyle.*

So many gods, so many creeds,
  So many paths that wind and wind;
  When just the art of being kind
Is all the sad world needs.
—*Ella Wheeler Wilcox.*

A little philosophy inclineth man's mind to atheism, but depth in philosophy bringeth men's minds about to religion. —*Bacon.*

The best fire doesna flare up the soonest.
—*George Eliot.*

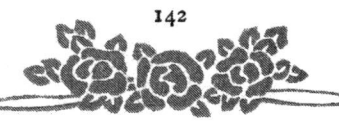

HELPS TO HAPPINESS

Thou goest thy way, and I go mine,
　Apart, yet not afar;
Only a thin veil hangs between
　The pathways where we are.
"God keep watch 'tween thee and me";
　This is my prayer;
He looketh thy way, He looketh mine,
　And keeps us near.

Although our paths be separate,
　And thy way is not mine,
Yet coming to the mercy-seat,
　My soul will meet with thine.
"God keep watch 'tween thee and me"
　I'll whisper there;
He blesseth thee, He blesseth me,
　And we are near.
　　　　　　　　　—Julia A. Baker.

HELPS TO HAPPINESS

We sleep, but the loom of life never stops; and the pattern which was weaving when the sun went down is weaving when it comes up to-morrow. —*Henry Ward Beecher.*

If thou wilt fill thy brain with Boston and New York, with fashion and covetousness, and wilt stimulate thy jaded senses with wine and French coffee, thou shalt find no radiance of wisdom in the lonely waste of the pine-woods.
—*Emerson.*

No matter about yesterday's shortcomings, to-day is yours. —*Annie H. Ryder.*

It's easy finding reasons why other folks should be patient. —*George Eliot.*

"Swift kindnesses are best; a long delay in kindness takes the kindness all away."

HELPS TO HAPPINESS

Resolved, to live with all my might while I do live; Resolved, never to lose one moment of time, but improve it in the most profitable way I possibly can; Resolved, never to do anything which I should despise or think meanly of in another; Resolved, never to do anything out of revenge; Resolved, never to do anything which I should be afraid to do if it were the last hour of my life. —*Jonathan Edwards.*

HELPS TO HAPPINESS

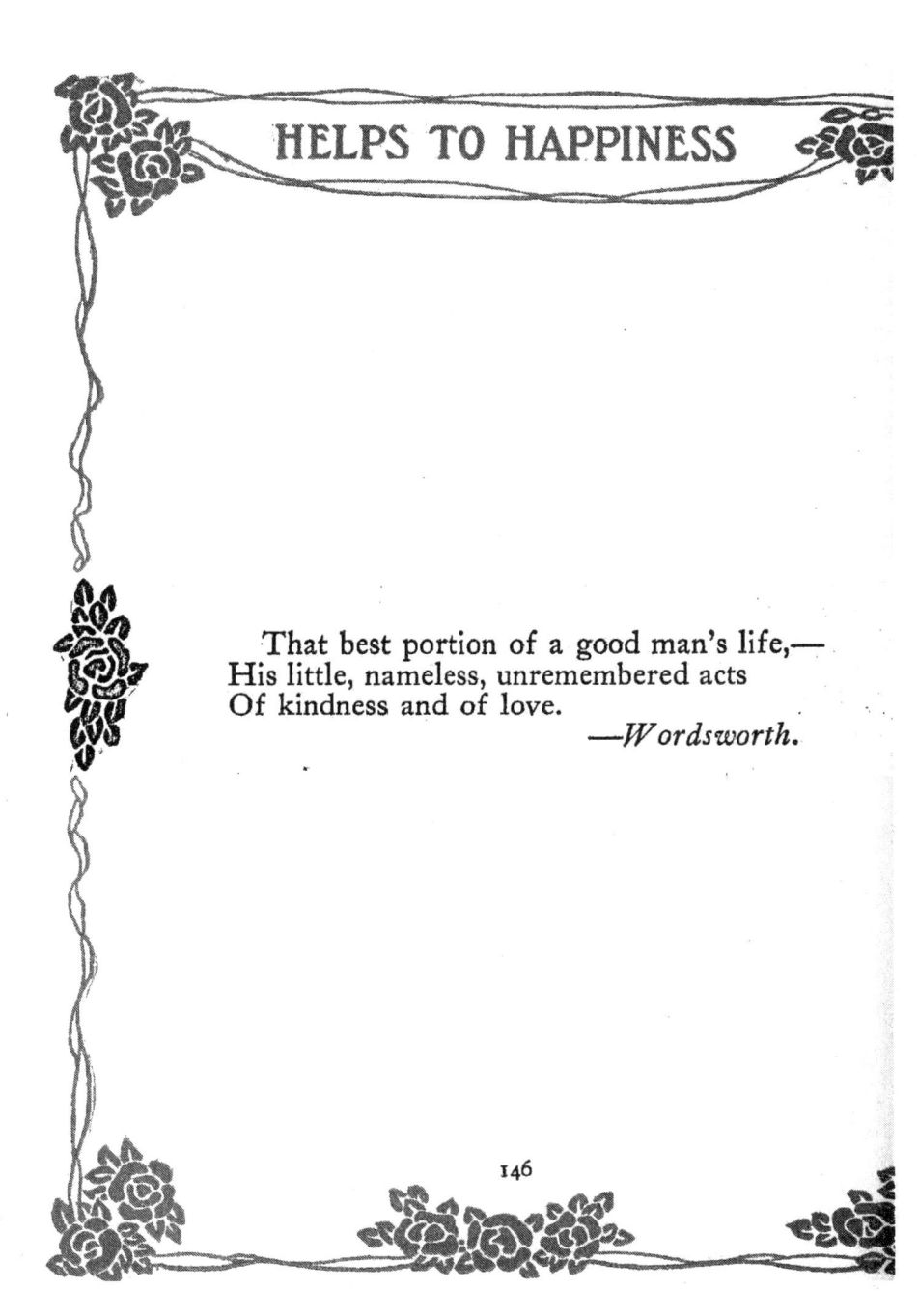

That best portion of a good man's life,—
His little, nameless, unremembered acts
Of kindness and of love.
—*Wordsworth.*

HELPS TO HAPPINESS

Who taught the raven in a drought to throw pebbles into a hollow tree where she espied water, that the water might rise so as she might come to it? Who taught the bee to sail through such a vast sea of air, and to find the way from a flower in a field to her hive? Who taught the ant to bite every grain of corn that she burieth in her hill, lest it should take root and grow?

—*Bacon.*

A good deed is never lost; he who shows courtesy, reaps friendship; and he who plants kindness, gathers love.   —*Basil.*

A man who lives right, and is right, has more power in his silence than another has by his words. Character is like bells which ring out sweet music, and which, when touched accidentally even, resound with sweet music.

—*Phillips Brooks.*

Beyond all doing of good is the being good; for he that is good not only does good things, but all that he does is good.

—*George MacDonald.*

HELPS TO HAPPINESS

Circumstances! I make circumstances.
—*Napoleon I.*

Infinite toil would not enable you to sweep away a mist; but, by ascending a little, you may often look over it altogether.
—*Arthur Helps.*

A little thought will sometimes prevent you from being discontented at not meeting with the gratitude which you have expected. If you were only to measure your expectations of gratitude by the extent of benevolence which you have expended, you would seldom have occasion to call people ungrateful.
—*Arthur Helps.*

"To say well is good, but to do well is better. Do well is the spirit, and say well, the letter."

Discontent is want of self-reliance; it is infirmity of will.
—*Emerson.*

If your name is to live at all, it is so much more to have it live in people's hearts than only in their brains. I don't know that one's eyes fill with tears when he thinks of the famous inventor of logarithms.
—*Holmes.*

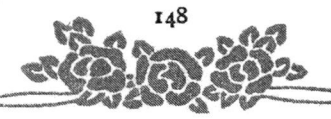

HELPS TO HAPPINESS

To live in the presence of great truths and eternal laws — that is what keeps a man patient when the world ignores him and calm and unspoiled when the world praises him

— Balzac

HELPS TO HAPPINESS

"Men are usually tempted by the devil, but an idle man positively tempts the devil."

"Silence, or neglect, dissolves many friendships."

"Friendship supplies the place of everything to those who know how to make the right use of it; it makes your prosperity more happy, and it makes your adversity more easy."

"It may be true that a rolling stone gathers no moss, but who desires to become moss-covered, anyway?"

If you wish success in life, make perseverance your bosom friend, experience your wise counsellor, caution your elder brother, and hope your guardian genius. —*Addison.*

HELPS TO HAPPINESS

We shall reap such joys in the by and by,
   But what have we sown to-day?
We shall build us mansions in the sky,
   But what have we built to-day?
'Tis sweet in idle dreams to bask,
But here and now do we do our task?
Yes, this is the thing our souls must ask—
   "What have we done to-day?"
                  —*Nixon Waterman.*

HELPS TO HAPPINESS

HAPPINESS.

If thou workest at that which is before thee, following right reason seriously, vigorously, calmly, without allowing anything else to distract thee, but keeping thy divine part pure, if thou shouldst be bound to give it back immediately; if thou holdest to this, expecting nothing, fearing nothing, but satisfied with thy present activity according to nature, and with heroic truth in every word and sound which thou utterest, thou wilt live happy. And there is no man who is able to prevent this.

—*Marcus Aurelius.*

HELPS TO HAPPINESS

We live in deeds, not years; in thoughts, not breaths;
In feelings, not in figures on a dial,
We should count time by heart throbs, He most lives
Who thinks most, feels the noblest, acts the best.

There is a necessary limit to our achievement, but none to our attempt.
—*Phillips Brooks.*

It is not the going out of port, but the coming in, that determines the success of a voyage.
—*Henry Ward Beecher.*

The secret of success in life is for a man to be ready for his opportunity when it comes.
—*Disraeli.*

HELPS TO HAPPINESS

And so I find it well to come
For deeper rest to this still room;
For here the habit of the soul
Feels less the outer world's control.
And from the silence, multiplied,
By these still forms on every side,
The world that time and sense has known
Falls off and leaves us God alone.

—John G. Whittier.

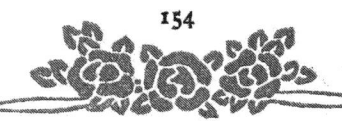

HELPS TO HAPPINESS

A wrong-doer is often a man that has left something undone, not always he that has done something. —*Marcus Aurelius.*

The truest self-respect is not to think of self.
—*Henry Ward Beecher.*

It is a sad weakness in us, after all, that the thought of a man's death hallows him anew to us; as if life were not sacred too—as if it were comparatively a light thing to fail in love and reverence to the brother who has to climb the whole toilsome steep with us, and all our tears and tenderness were due to the one who is spared that hard journey. —*George Eliot.*

The test of your Christian character should be that you are a joy-bearing agent to the world.
—*Henry Ward Beecher.*

"To-day is your opportunity, to-morrow some other fellow's."

HELPS TO HAPPINESS

"Now is the time; ah, friend, no longer wait
To scatter loving smiles and words of cheer
To those around whose lives are now so dear.
They may not meet you in the coming year.
  Now is the time."

HELPS TO HAPPINESS

Lost—a golden hour, set with sixty diamond minutes. There is no reward, for it is gone forever. —*Henry Ward Beecher.*

HELPS TO HAPPINESS

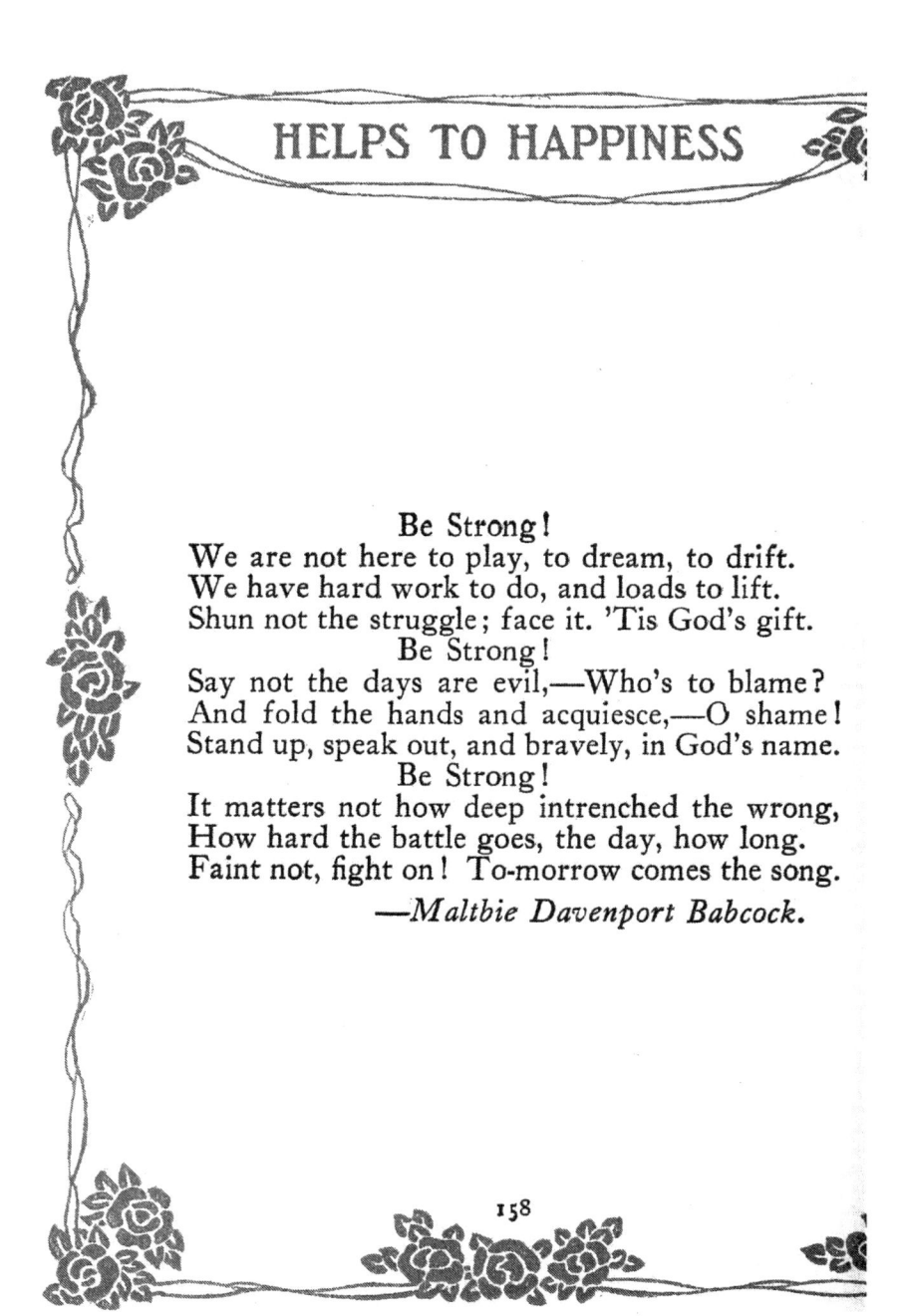

              Be Strong!
We are not here to play, to dream, to drift.
We have hard work to do, and loads to lift.
Shun not the struggle; face it. 'Tis God's gift.
              Be Strong!
Say not the days are evil,—Who's to blame?
And fold the hands and acquiesce,—O shame!
Stand up, speak out, and bravely, in God's name.
              Be Strong!
It matters not how deep intrenched the wrong,
How hard the battle goes, the day, how long.
Faint not, fight on! To-morrow comes the song.

              —*Maltbie Davenport Babcock.*

HELPS TO HAPPINESS

Nothing great was ever achieved without enthusiasm.
—*Emerson.*

"When the outlook is not good, try the uplook."

"It is easy enough to be pleasant
    When life flows along like a song;
But the man worth while is the one who can smile
    When everything goes dead wrong."

HELPS TO HAPPINESS

The soul grows into lovely habits as easily as into ugly ones, and the moment a life begins to blossom into beautiful words and deeds that moment a new standard of conduct is established and your eager neighbors look to you for a continuous manifestation of the good cheer, the sympathy, the ready wit, the comradeship, or the inspiration you once showed yourself capable of. Bear figs for a season or two and the world outside the orchard is very unwilling you should bear thistles. —*Kate Douglas Wiggin.*

Answer not a fool according to his folly, lest thou also be like unto him.
—*Proverbs* 26:4.

"The beauty of the house is order, the blessing of the house is contentment, the glory of the house is hospitality, the crown of the house is godliness."

"Let a man have firm faith that he is born to do some day what at the moment seems totally impossible and it is fifty to one that he does it before he dies—so great is the power of faith when applied to human endeavor."

A man often pays dear for a small frugality.
—*Emerson.*

HELPS TO HAPPINESS

Build a little fence of trust around to-day
Fill the space with loving deeds and therein stay
Look not through the sheltering bars upon to-morrow
God will help thee bear what comes of joy or sorrow

—Mary Frances Butts

HELPS TO HAPPINESS

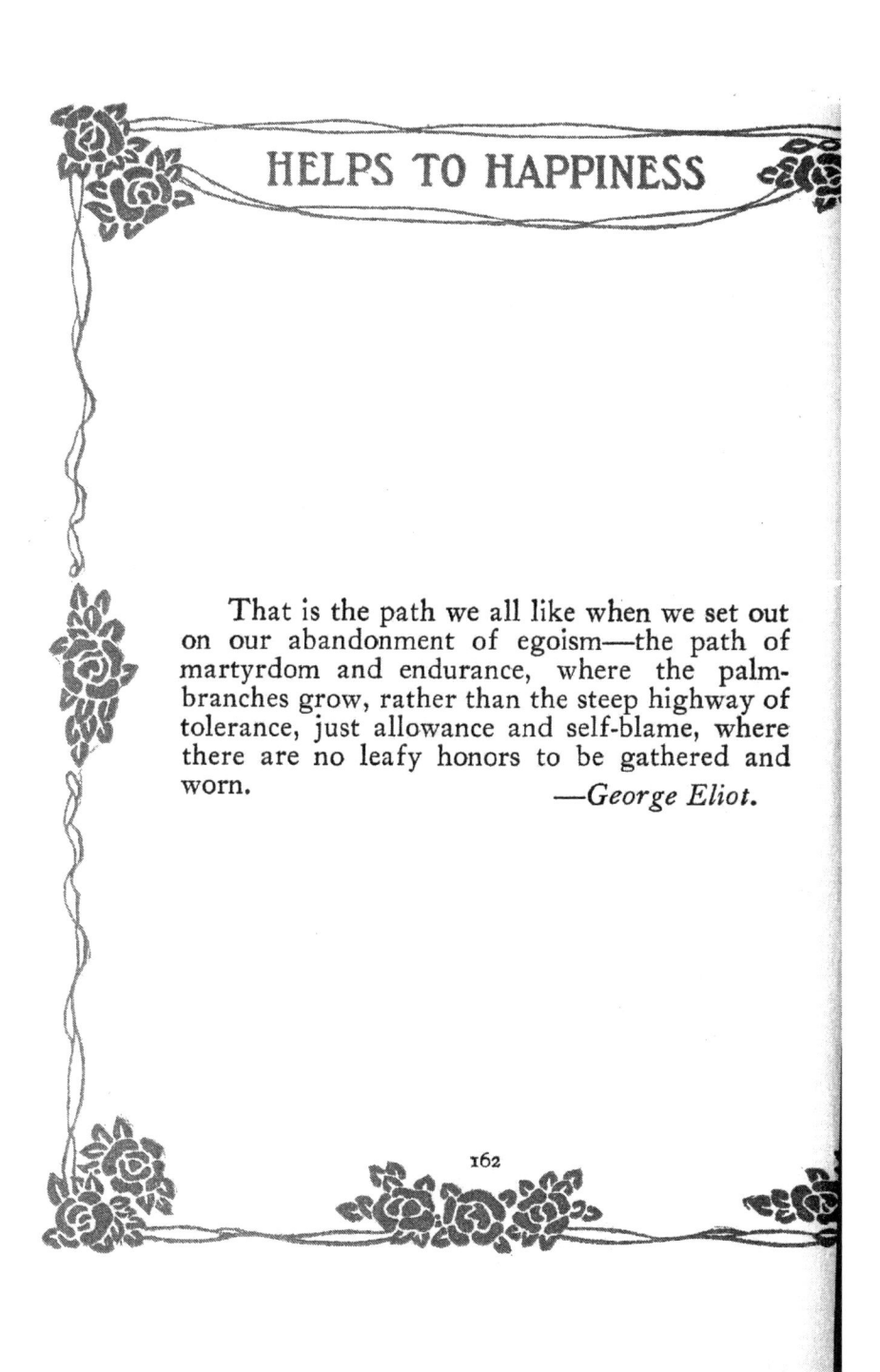

That is the path we all like when we set out on our abandonment of egoism—the path of martyrdom and endurance, where the palm-branches grow, rather than the steep highway of tolerance, just allowance and self-blame, where there are no leafy honors to be gathered and worn.
—*George Eliot.*

HELPS TO HAPPINESS

If any little word of ours can make one life the brighter;
If any little song of ours can make one heart the lighter;
God help us speak that little word, and take our bit of singing,
And drop it in some lonely vale, and set the echoes ringing.

HELPS TO HAPPINESS

"Hark, friends, it strikes! the year's last hour:
  A solemn sound to hear.
Come fill the cup and let us pour
  Our blessings on the parting year.
The years that were, the dim, the gray,
  Receive this night with choral hymn
A sister shade as lost as they
  And soon to be as gray and dim.
Fill high. She brought us both of weal and woe
And nearer lies the land to which we go."

HELPS TO HAPPINESS

Here you stand at the parting of the ways; some road you are to take; and as you stand here, consider and know how it is that you intend to live. Carry no bad habits, no corrupting associations, no enmities and strifes into this New Year. Leave these behind, and let the dead Past bury its dead; leave them behind, and thank God that you are able to leave them.
—*Ephraim Peabody.*

HELPS TO HAPPINESS

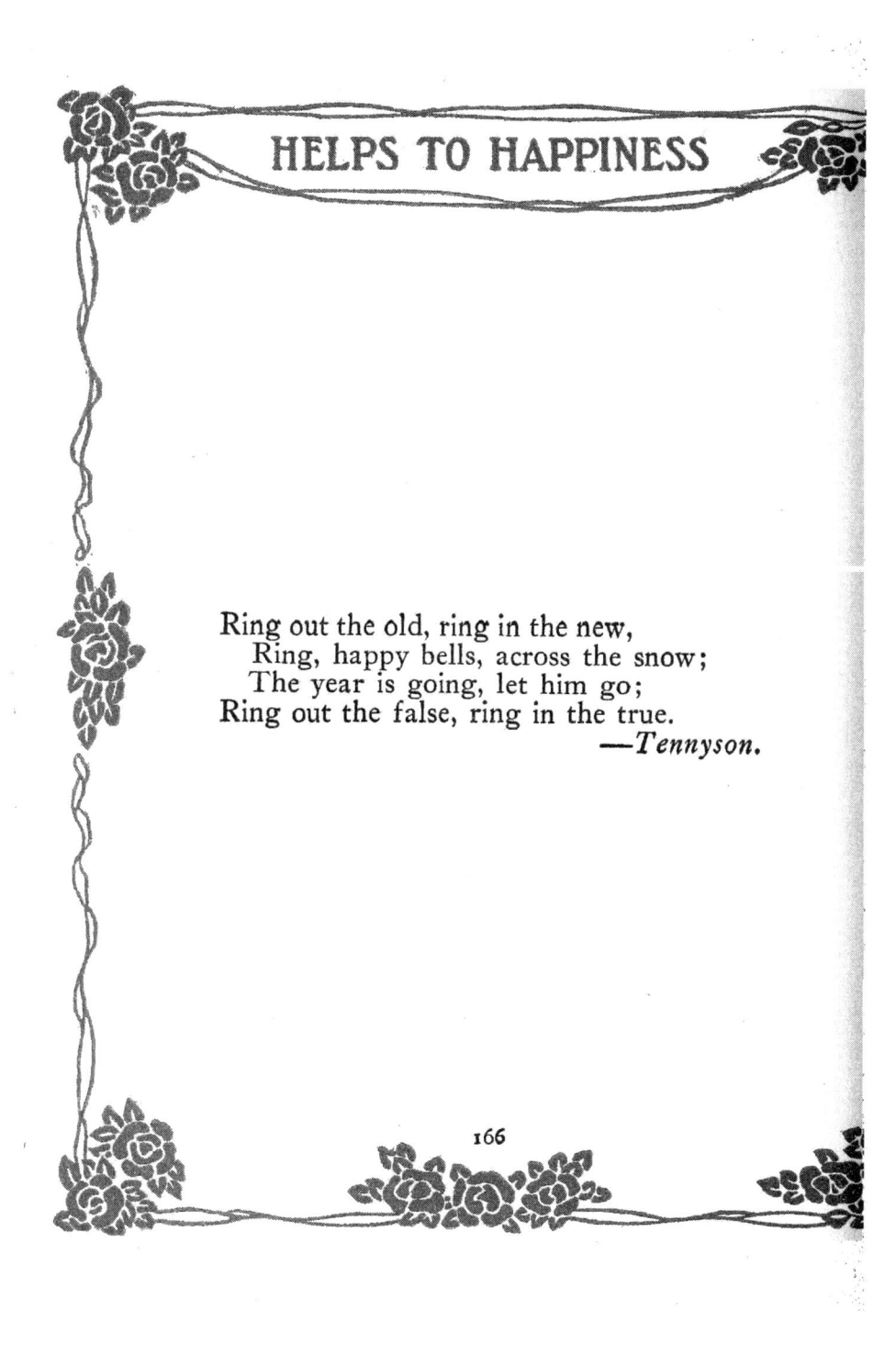

Ring out the old, ring in the new,
　Ring, happy bells, across the snow;
　The year is going, let him go;
Ring out the false, ring in the true.
—*Tennyson.*

HELPS TO HAPPINESS

INDEX

Addison	122, 150
Arabian Proverb	98
Arnold, Edwin	35, 42, 83
Aurelius, Marcus	73, 106, 137, 152, 155
Babcock, Maltbie Davenport	158
Bacon, Lord	54, 90, 113, 142, 147
Baker, Julia A.	143
Balzac	149
Basil	147
Beecher, Henry Ward	5, 12, 34, 40, 54, 83, 90, 96, 113, 129, 130, 137, 139, 144, 153, 155, 157
Billings, Josh	9, 18, 96
Black, Hugh	80, 83
Boveé	33
Bridges, M.	47
Brooks, Phillips	24, 30, 33, 53, 67, 77, 81, 95, 96, 117, 120, 123, 133, 147, 153
Browning, Elizabeth Barrett	46, 52, 106, 116
Browning, Robert	12, 14, 39, 53, 58, 65, 69, 70, 71, 105
Bulwer (Lord Lytton)	114
Bunyan, John	40, 56, 64
Burroughs, John	62
Burton, Richard	57
Butts, Mary Frances	55, 161
Byron, Lord	33
Carey, P.	40, 128
Carlyle, Thomas	12, 24, 30, 34, 51, 56, 75, 110, 118, 140, 142
Carnegie, Andrew	127
Chalmers	130, 138
Chadwick, John White	88
Channing, William Henry	87

HELPS TO HAPPINESS

Chesterfield, Lord 131
Cicero 101
Clarendon, Lord 27
Clarke, James Freeman 22
Child, L. M. 86
Cowper 63, 70
Cooke, Edmund Vance 109, 125
Davis, Ozora Stearns 86
De Sales, St. Francis 80
Dickens, Charles 21, 27, 70, 71, 88, 100
Disraeli 153
Drummond, Henry 82, 90, 139
Du Maurier, George 117
Edwards, Jonathan 145
Eliot, George, 12, 22, 24, 31, 90 117, 118, 136, 142, 144, 155, 162
Emerson, Ralph Waldo 10, 12, 13, 31, 75, 80, 96, 97, 118,
 125, 126, 129, 144, 148, 159, 160
Epictetus 41, 53, 58, 114
Faber, F. W. 99
Farrar, Canon 14
Fenelon 110
Fields, J. T. 95
Fleming, Paul 58, 94
Franklin, Benjamin 14, 53, 104, 110
French 40
Froude, James Anthony 12, 53, 56
Fuller, T. 33
Gladstone, W. E. 40, 50
Goethe 48, 56, 108, 115, 135
Gough, John B. 141
Hale, Edward Everett 132
Haliburton 16
Hamilton, Alexander 111

HELPS TO HAPPINESS

Hamilton, James	136
Hamilton, Anna E.	48
Hamilton, Gail	142
Harmsworth, Alfred	34
Hegeman, A. B.	21, 37
Helps, Arthur	16, 48, 108, 133, 140, 148
Henley, W. E.	48
Hepworth, George H.	75
Hill, James J.	26, 119, 127
Hodges, Leigh Mitchell	25
Holland, J. G.	36, 43, 124
Holmes, Oliver W.	46, 122, 148
Hood, Thomas	98
Hughes, Thomas	15, 42, 60, 77, 120
Hugo, Victor	75
Ingelow, Jean	124
Johnson, Samuel	44, 60
Jefferson, Thomas	128
Jerome, J. K.	100
Kempis, Thomas á	14
Ken, Bishop	54
Kingsley, Charles	60, 102, 124
Knapp, Lillian	14
Kipling, Rudyard	84, 90
Landor, W. S.	63
Larcom, Lucy	129
La Rochefoucauld	70
Lincoln, Abraham	22, 29, 66, 87, 107, 113
Longfellow, Henry W.	92, 100, 109, 110, 114, 116, 121, 125
Lorimer, George Horace	20, 70
Lowell, James Russell	98, 101
Lubbock, John	61, 87
Mabie, Hamilton Wright	20, 25, 69, 100

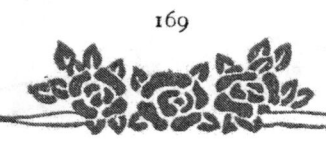

169

MacDonald, George . . . 16, 60, 69, 104, 128, 147
Maclaren, Ian 46, 61
Marden, Orison Swett 122
Mason, C. A. 77
Manutius, Aldus Pius 33
Mathews, William 31
Meredith, Owen 17
Micah 128
Montaigne 140
Moody, D. L. 48
Morgan, Angela 45
Mulock, Dinah Maria 127
Napoleon I 16, 123, 148
Paine, Thomas 46
Patmore, Coventry 123
Peabody, Ephraim 165
Peace, W. S. 24
Penn, William 66, 73
Plato 22
Porter 93
Potter, Henry C. 95
Procter, A. 111
Pusey, E. B. 91, 95
Quincy, Josiah 66
Quarles, F. 72
Richardson 22
Richter 66, 71
Robertson, F. W. 22, 88, 92
Rockefeller, John D. 28
Roosevelt, Theodore 20, 21, 27, 61, 63, 67, 68, 75, 86, 87, 98
Ruskin, John . . 14, 27, 36, 41, 51, 54, 59, 102, 110, 137
Ryan, Father 118
Ryder, Annie H. 144

HELPS TO HAPPINESS

Scandinavian Proverb	73
Scott, Walter	20, 83
Seneca	69
Sertorius	102
Shakespeare, William	20, 25, 63, 67, 86, 96, 105
Shaw, Leslie M.	18, 60, 61, 67, 86, 92
Sheridan, Thomas	122
Sidney, Philip	18, 67
Smiles, Samuel	16, 24, 108, 136
Socrates	36, 51
Solomon	13
Southey	13
Spencer, Herbert	114
Stevenson, Robert Louis	7, 40, 42, 45, 46, 58, 59, 79, 106
Stetson, Charlotte Perkins	76
Story, W. W.	42, 74
Swing, David	56
Sumner, Charles	41
Swett	106
Syrus, Publius	41
Thackeray	41
Tennyson, Alfred	166
Thoreau, Henry David	17, 52, 113, 138, 140
Tullock	13
Van Dyke, Henry	10, 18, 36, 38, 48, 108, 124, 134, 140
Vincent, John H.	10
Wagner, Charles	34, 134, 138
Ward, Artemus	75
Ware, J. F. W.	105, 128
Washington, George	34, 138
Waterman, Nixon	120, 151
Wayland, H. L.	83
Webster, Daniel	137

HELPS TO HAPPINESS

Whitman, M. B.	19
Whittier, John G.	73, 112, 139, 154
Wiggin, Kate Douglass	160
Wilcox, Ella Wheeler	142
Williams, Roger	90
Wise, Henry D.	106
Wordsworth	136, 146
Young, Edward	17

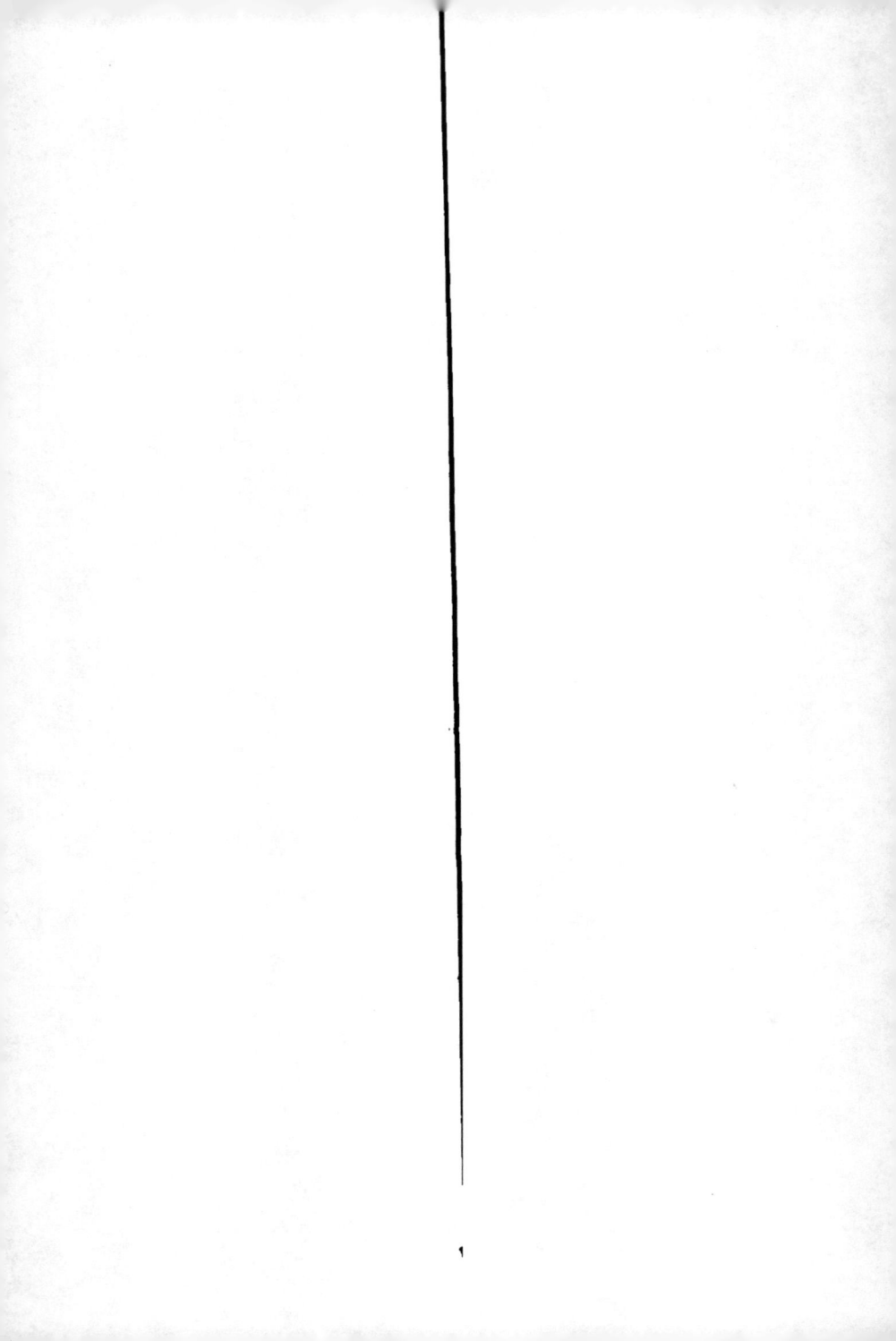

But Once

I shall pass through this world but once. Any good, therefore, that I can do, or any kindness that I can show to any human being, let me do it now. Let me not defer or neglect it, for I shall not pass this way again.

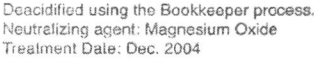